The Medieval Religious Stage

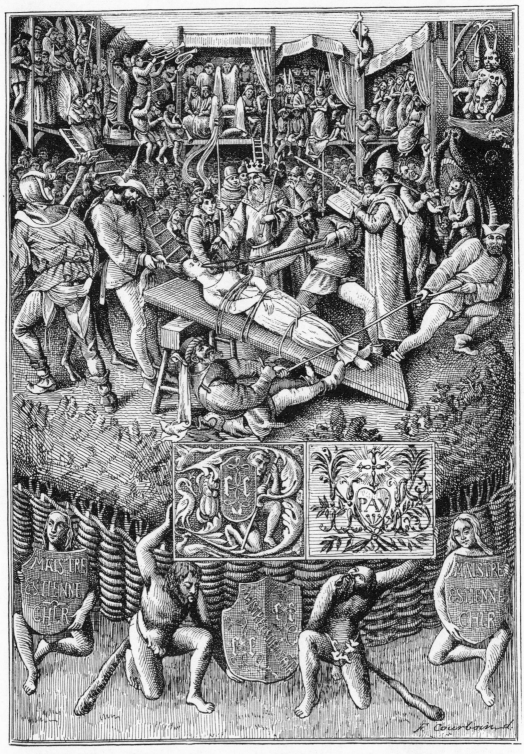

Jean Fouquet's miniature *The Martyrdom of St. Apollonia,* painted for the *Livre d'Heures pour maître Etienne Chevalier* (ca. 1452–56). From Germain Bapst, *Essai sur l'histoire du théâtre* (Paris 1893), still the clearest available reproduction.

The Medieval Religious Stage

Shapes and Phantoms

A. M. NAGLER

New Haven and London   Yale University Press   1976

Published with assistance from the Mary Cady Tew Memorial Fund.

Library of Congress catalog card number: 75-43328
International standard book number: 0-300-01986-6

Designed by John O. C. McCrillis
and set in Garamond type.
Printed in the United States of America by
Murray Printing Company, Westford, Massachusetts.

Published in Great Britain, Europe, Africa, and Asia (except Japan)
by Yale University Press, Ltd., London.
Distributed in Latin America by Kaiman & Polon,
Inc., New York City; in Australia and New Zealand by Book & Film
Services, Artarmon, N.S.W., Australia; in Japan by
John Weatherhill, Inc., Tokyo.

This book was originally written in German. It
was translated by George C. Schoolfield.

To my doctoral students
1946–1976

Contents

Illustrations

Prelude

THE FOLLOWING GLOSSES on the problems of theater history with which the Middle Ages challenge the latterday observer are partly a research report and partly a call for a more stringent treatment of the extant material and a sharper focus of the scholarly lense.

Our investigations are based on the premise that it is the task of the theater historian to reconstruct past styles of performance. No period is better suited than the Middle Ages to train students for work in the field of theatrical scholarship in general.

The theater historian is not concerned with the restoration of the text; ceding this difficult task to qualified philologists, he employs the best available text and, above all, its explicit or implicit stage directions. Nor is the theater historian concerned with the transformations which the figure of Mary Magdalene has undergone. Nor does he make comparisons among the variants of Resurrection scenes. For him, it is a matter of indifference if the *mercator* merely has a shrewish wife or if he also has a *servus* who introduces smut to a greater or lesser degree into the sacred action. We are engaged neither in historical philology nor in the study of literature, neither in folklore nor in sociology. The styles of performance and their more or less plausible reconstructions, these are our primary concern, and I shall be honored if this be called a purist's stance.

In our work we depend upon sources which for the most part are tightlipped indeed. (We are provided with an optimum situation but once, in the case of the Lucerne *Osterspiel* in 1583.) We cannot take recourse to photographs or to promptbooks (in the present-day meaning); at best we have enigmatic directors' registers (*Dirigierrollen*). The opinions of the press cannot enlighten or confuse us. Contemporary eyewitness accounts exist only in the singular case of Florence. Why, then, have generations of scholars toiled over the medieval theater? A kind of curiosity drives us on, the desire to test the keenness of our minds against the scarce and imperfectly transmitted materials of the Middle Ages. Seen from the point of view of pure scholarship, our endeavors in the majority of cases are hopeless. Below we shall have the opportunity to speak of such desperate attempts. The medieval theater is a field of research which should teach us to recognize the limitations of our knowledge, or, more precisely, the limitations of what we may surmise. Again and again, we ought to be admonished to proceed with caution, in the event we are inclined to work impressionistically with undemonstrable assertions.

The study of the medieval theater requires a universal point of view. We cannot afford to be students of German or English or Romance matters alone. The boundaries of language must fall.

The choice of problems to be treated in the following text is both arbitrary and fragmentary, and places no value on a chronological scheme. Here, we are dealing in paradigms, or "Modelle," of the sort currently employed in the academic trade. As a matter of fact, the commentaries on available performance reconstructions presented in this book have arisen out of seminar exercises which I developed with my students in the course of my thirty years as a teacher at Yale University. Thus opinions are also taken into account which have been worked out in seminar courses by the doctoral candidates of our speciality. As a result, the following observations form a kind of "Studienausgabe."

A. M. N.

1 Toying with Rubrics

AT THE OUTSET, our survey will concentrate on plays for which we possess only the text, accompanied by more or less detailed stage directions. There is no archival material extant; thus we do not know in what city or on what site the performance took place. We have no stage plans, and no other pictorial evidence. The rubrics are our primary and sole aid in reconstructing the production style. And so, let us play the game of rubrics. It is entertaining for the researcher, though it may sometimes be harmful to his scholarly health.

"LE MYSTÈRE D'ADAM"

As a point of departure let us choose a text (from the twelfth century) which provides us with rubrics aplenty, the Anglo-Norman *Jeu d'Adam*. A number of scholars have already gone to great pains in reconstructing its stage—Paul Studer, Karl Grass, Gustave Cohen, Grace Frank, Uda Ebel, and Wolfgang Greisenegger.[1]

Here we have both certain knowledge and more uncertainties. No doubts exist about the background: the performance took place before the portal of a church. Yet the uncertainties begin directly: which portal are we talking about? The main portal, on the west, offers itself as a first possibility; but Miss Frank cannot agree, for, in the course of the play, there was singing (in Latin) in the choir of the church. Could listeners, standing before the main portal, have heard these songs distinctly? Thus she proposes the entrance to the southern transept of the (unidentifiable) church: here, the public would have been nearer to the songs which resounded in the choir.[2] Whether it was the west or south portal, I see no need for conjectures here, as long as we are in the dark about far more essential matters.

It is certain that God the Father (*Figura*) emerged several times from the church's

---

1. Paul Studer, ed., *Le Mystère d'Adam, an Anglo-Norman Drama of the Twelfth Century* (Manchester, 1918). Karl Grass, ed., *Das Adamsspiel, Anglo-normannisches Mysterium des XII. Jahrhunderts*, 3rd rev. ed. (Halle, 1928). Gustave Cohen, *Histoire de la mise en scène dans le théâtre religieux du Moyen Age* (Paris, 1926), pp. 51–62. Grace Frank, "Genesis and Staging of the *Jeu d'Adam*," *PMLA* 59 (1944): 7–17. Uda Ebel, ed., *Das Altfranzösische Adamsspiel* (Munich, 1968). Wolfgang Greisenegger, "Religiöses Schauspiel als politisches Instrument: Beobachtungen am altfranzösischen Adamsspiel," *Maske und Kothurn* 21 (1975): 1–32.

2. We should not exclude the possibility that *in choro* refers not to a location within the church but to a choir singing the lectio in the narthex. See Ebel, *Das Altfranzösische Adamsspiel*, p. 116, n. 40.

interior and went back to it again; this was the "umbilical cord" which, as Sainte-Beuve expressed it, connected the newborn drama with the mother church. It is certain, furthermore, that there were mansions for the Terrestrial Paradise and for Hell. We are even provided with details about the makeup of Paradise, something which rubrics ordinarily do not furnish. The Paradise was partially concealed by silk curtains, interlaced (*serantur,* according to Paul Aebischer's emendation) with *odoriferi flores et frondes;* only the heads of the actors and the tops of the planted fruit trees were to be seen. The first rubric suggests that Paradise be erected on a *loco eminenciori.* Studer and Cohen immediately envisioned stairs and ladders, but Miss Frank has rejected the idea of scaffolding of this sort, since there is no mention of climbing up or down anywhere in the stage directions. The "elevated place" was simply the terrace before the entrance to the church, presumably with stairs ascending to it. The dimensions of Paradise are not available; but since Adam and Eve strolled around in Paradise, admiring its beauties, the *locus* may have been of fair size. The following scenes, the loss of Paradise and the Cain-and-Abel episode, may have been acted on a lower plane, the *platea.* A part of this plane was designated as the "field," which Adam and Eve tilled by the sweat of their brows while the Devil sowed thorns and thistles upon it. On this platea, probably, there also stood the two great stones which the brothers used for their sacrifices. Later Cain and Abel went "ad locus remotum et quasi secretum," where the fratricide occurred. It is not clear what was meant by this "distant and secret place." Greisenegger[3] speaks of separate "houses" for Abel and Cain. Such are not called for in the rubrics. The brothers simply have "loca sua," the equivalent of the German *Standorte.*

I cannot agree with Greisenegger who, influenced by Auerbach, discovered in the play a "realistische Grundhaltung." On the contrary, the stage directions point to a rather conventional, formal acting style. The presentational gestures (beating the breast and thigh as expressions of grief, the persistent pointing to Paradise) and the instruction "to speak composedly" and to pronounce everything clearly are in accord with the liturgical choral chanting emerging from the church. The pot hidden under Abel's garment does not serve as a handy device for stage bloodshed but rather as a cushion against Cain's blow. We have not yet reached the stage of "bloody" realism.

A bench ("scamnum")—perhaps the special seat of the celebrant—was required for the prophets; seated on it, they delivered their quotations from scripture. They had prepared themselves for their appearance in a "loco secreto." Bileam rode in on his she-ass. It may well be thought that Hell, with its smoke and the clanging pots and

---

3. "Religiöses Schauspiel," p. 10.

pans, was at ground level, especially since the Devil once makes his way through the spectators ("per populum"). On other occasions, too, the devils ran "per plateas." While most interpreters have rendered *platea* as "square," we do not wish to exclude the possibility that it indicated a podium, which had been built over the stairs leading to the entrance of the church.[4]

Thus we have reached the limits of permissible conjecture. The result: even abundant rubrics will produce only vague notions. Karl Grass is among those who have been disappointed: "As far as the question of the structure of the stage is concerned, the stage directions leave us in the lurch.... A reconstruction of the stage, as it was intended for the play, is scarcely possible on the basis of these particulars."[5]

"La Seinte Resurreccion"

We possess the fragment of an Anglo-Norman Resurrection play, *La Seinte Resurreccion,* from the end of the twelfth century.[6] The fragment exists in two manuscripts, an older one from Canterbury and the later so-called Paris version. The extant portions begin with a scene in which Joseph of Arimathea asks permission to bury the body of Christ. The Canterbury fragment ends with the arrest of Joseph, who must answer to Pilate for his actions.

The theater historian will be interested, before all else, by the prologue to the Paris version,[7] which—in its verses—presents the various scenes of action to the spectators. The speaker declares that he would like, first of all, to enumerate "les lius e les mansions," and begins ("primerement") with the cross. Then, beside it ("puis après") the *monumentum.* A prison is necessary, too, in which Nicodemus will be shut up later on. Hell is likewise in this part ("de cele part") of the stage. Heaven is "del altre part." Next there is an enumeration of six places which the prologue characterizes as "estals," that is, scaffolds. The order of succession is as follows: (1) Pilate with his six or seven vassals, (2) a station for Caiaphas and the Jews, (3) a location for Joseph of Arimathea and his six followers, (4) a place for Nicodemus and his six companions, (5) a place of assembly for the disciples of Jesus, (6) the three Marys. The spectators are requested to imagine Galilee and Emmaus "en mi la place."

To my knowledge, three attempts have been made to arrive at a stage plan on the

---

4. Ebel, *Das Altfranzösische Adamsspiel,* p. 57, identifies *platea* with *Kirchplatz.*
5. *Das Adamsspiel,* p. xxiii.
6. See the edition by Jean Gray Wright, *La Résurrection du Sauveur* (Paris, 1931).
7. Published by L. Petit de Julleville, *Les Mystères* (Paris, 1880), 1:92; also by O. B. Hardison, Jr., *Christian Rite and Christian Drama in the Middle Ages* (Baltimore, 1965), p. 263.

basis of these pieces of information. Chambers[8] forces the localities into the ground plan of a church, and, over and beyond that, takes recourse to the plan of the Villingen play. He could not have misunderstood the prologue more thoroughly. Before we begin to discuss the two other reconstructions, by Jean Wright and O. B. Hardison, attention should be called to the fact that the prologue does not speak of a central location of the crucifix, but only mentions it first ("primerement"). The central position in a Resurrection play belongs to the monumentum, which stood at the center of the action from the *depositio* to the *visitatio* (which has not been preserved).

Miss Wright has placed the grave in the middle,[9] locating the prison and Hell at stage left and the cross and Heaven at stage right. It appears to be a reasonable arrangement. Less convincing is the grouping of the "estals," which Miss Wright puts in front of the row of mansions and parallel to it. Her "estals" thus deprive the spectators of a view of the mansions in the background.

Hardison's plan[10] moves the cross into the center. Otherwise, in his disposition of the mansions and the scaffolds, he works with "positional symbolism,"[11] by which he means (as I understand it) that the Christian party is to be lodged on the side of Heaven, and the opponents of Christ on the side of Hell. Nevertheless, Hardison fails to follow this principle when he puts the station of Pilate in the vicinity of Heaven and makes Joseph and Nicodemus into neighbors of Caiaphas. In order to realize that "symbolic positional plan" which Hardison pursues (Rueff's "Bedeutungsbühne"), the grave would have to assume the central position, and the cross would have to be placed at the point which Hardison has given over to the monumentum. Furthermore, Pilate and Joseph-Nicodemus ought to switch places. And so, to be sure, we arrive once again at that favorite trick: sleight of hand with rubrics.

The Canterbury fragment,[12] which offers some essential textual differences from the Paris version, likewise has a prologue, which changes the order of the mansions and the stage locations. In the first place, the speaker calls attention to the fact that the performance demands an "asez large place." Then, here too, he begins with the cross. "Beside it the grave." Now those persons are named who have a connection with the grave: the soldiers who guard it, the three Marys, who visit it. Then, an "estage" for the apostles is required. Nicodemus needs a "liu." The other persons

8. E. K. Chambers, *The Mediaeval Stage* (Oxford, 1903), 2:83.
9. *La Résurrection du Sauveur*, p. cxix.
10. *Christian Rite and Christian Drama*, p. 266.
11. Ibid., p. 265.
12. Likewise edited by Miss Wright.

are listed without any further indication of their position: Joseph of Arimathea, Pilate and his knights, Caiaphas, Annas, and the Jews. Next, a "tower of David" is mentioned and a character named Bartholomeus, not otherwise identified. Now the prologue returns to the mansions, to the prison, to Hell, "where the foes are and the ancient fathers, lying in chains," to Heaven, "where the angels dwell." Galilee is "en mi la place," as in the Paris version. Emmaus is described as "un petit chastel."

The play consists of short scenes, which are connected by narrative transitional texts. It cannot be determined whether these connecting links, which are in verse, are to be regarded as stage directions, or were spoken by the *meneur de jeu.* If we lean toward the notion of a "demonstrative" director, then this "epic" technique can appear to us to be a prefiguration of what Thornton Wilder so successfully undertook in *Our Town,* where he had his stage manager not only introduce the public to the *loca* (indicated only in a symbolic way) of a small town in New Hampshire, but also gave him the task of establishing the connections between the various scenes.

"CONVERSIO BEATI PAULI" (FLEURY)

The Latin *Conversion of Saint Paul* in the Fleury Collection[13] (twelfth or thirteenth century) may very well have been composed for a church performance, perhaps on the Feast of Saint Paul's Conversion (January 25).[14] The stage directions clearly reveal a polyscenic principle of staging, even though they are not sufficient for a realization of a plan of the various *sedes.* The first rubric requires that they be placed "in competenti loco," and, as a matter of fact, in such a way that Jerusalem and Damascus are separated by considerable space from one another. In Jerusalem, one sedes was reserved for the high priest, another for a young man who had the task of acting the role of Saul and who was surrounded by knights. "Aliquantulum longe" from these loca was Damascus, with three sedes, one for a man by the name of Judas, another for the head of the Synagogue, and, between them, a bed. A later stage direction provides for a wall ("quasi a muro"), from which Paul is lowered in a basket during his flight. Christ does not have a fixed location. He may have made his entrance from the sacristy, in order to give the blinded Saul the command to go to Damascus. He then turns to Ananias, while Saul is led to Judas. After his flight from Damascus, Paul returns to Jerusalem, where Barnabas brings him to the

13. Text in Karl Young, *The Drama of the Medieval Church* (Oxford, 1933), 2:219–22.
14. Grace Frank, *The Medieval French Drama* (Oxford, 1954), p. 44, tends to believe that the Fleury plays originated in the monastery of S.-Benoit-sur-Loire.

apostles, who likewise have not been given a location in the rubrics. When Karl Young speaks of the "generosity" of the stage directions, we canot conceal our disappointment: they are by no means sufficient for a valid reconstruction.

THE SAINT GALLEN PASSION PLAY

The manuscript of 1,592 verses, from the fourteenth century, was most recently edited by Eduard Hartl.[15] In a separate essay,[16] Hartl then addressed himself to the question of the conditions of performance. Several attempts to make a stage plan exist; they simply bear witness, once again, to our basic helplessness in those cases where we have nothing save the text, and its rubrics, at our disposal. Scholarship is in agreement on but a single point: the play was performed in a church.

The three-story stage, envisioned by Emil Wolter,[17] has long since been rejected by Julius Petersen[18] as a figment of the imagination. Casting a final glance at Wolter's phantom stage: it postulated the existence of a choir, raised several feet above the nave of the church, a crypt for the scenes in Hell, and a gallery, running around the choir, for the Terrestial Paradise. Petersen doubted that a church constructed in this fashion existed in the Wetterau, the homeland of our play. In Petersen we find a spatial reduction, just as we do in Walther Müller's work: a play "for very limited spatial conditions" (Petersen[19]); "The stage appears to have encompassed only a quite small space, inside the church, without stage structures of any sort" (Müller[20]). In opposition to this proposal there is Eduard Hartl's opinion: "The crowd of actors—resulting from the wealth of scenes—requires a large number of very spacious mansions; thus we must assume the existence of about sixteen *loca*."[21] While Hartl had no particular formation in mind for these sixteen stage locations, Müller beheld the actors grouped, "no doubt, in a half circle around the stage.... The actors stepped forward from their places and sang or spoke their parts."[22] In the center of Müller's dream stage there stood a strange "prop, which at one and the same time could serve for the Last Supper, the grave of Lazarus, and the grave of the

---

15. *Das Benediktbeurer Passionsspiel, das St. Galler Passionsspiel* (Halle, 1952).

16. "Untersuchungen zum St. Galler Passionsspiel," in *Festschrift für Wolfgang Stammler.* (Berlin and Bielefeld, 1953), pp. 109–29.

17. Emil Wolter, ed., *Das St. Galler Spiel vom Leben Jesu* (Breslau, 1912).

18. "Aufführungen und Bühnenplan des älteren Frankfurter Passionsspieles," *Zeitschrift für deutsches Altertum,* 59 (1922) : 83–126; see esp. p. 95.

19. Ibid., p. 96.

20. Walther Müller, *Der schauspielerische Stil im Passionsspiel des Mittelalters* (Leipzig, 1927), p. 80.

21. Hartl, "Untersuchungen," p. 109.

22. *Der schauspielerische Stil,* p. 81.

Savior." Obviously, stage space could not have received more niggardly treatment than this. Müller took no notice of the Praetorium of Pontius Pilate, of the pinnacle of the Temple, of the mount of the temptation and the Mount of Olives. On this point Petersen allowed himself greater freedom. In case a raised choir was not available for the Praetorium, then a "small podium" could be set up in the transept; the pulpit could serve as the mount of the temptation, the high altar as the Mount of Olives, and Christ had the sacristy door at his disposal for that famous kick with which he burst open the gates of Hell ("pede trudat januam"). Petersen opted for a village church, "which could serve if need be."[23]

On the other hand, Hartl emphasized that the author or director, in his stage directions, proves himself to be a man of the theater through and through, a real professional. I should like to agree with him for once, and particularly with his opinion that the play makes quite extensive theatrical demands. When Hartl totted up sixteen loca, he came quite close to the truth of the matter. I distinguish among at least twelve clear-cut scenes of action, which cannot be argued out of existence by either Petersen or Müller, and which could even have been used in a village church. Furthermore, I do not regard it as being out of the question that a stage podium was erected, of the type for which evidence exists at this time in Avignon, where, in 1372, two podia were used simultaneously in the Franciscan church for the "Festum praesentationis beatae Mariae Virginis," staged by Philippe de Mézières.[24] A podium was put up in Bozen too, considerably later. In this latter case, to be sure, we are in the fortunate position of possessing Vigil Raber's stage plan, the ground plan of the church, plus archival evidence. If we did not have this documentation, no one would be convinced that the Bozen performance ever took place on a platform stage. This only in passing.

THE INNSBRUCK EASTER PLAY

In my opinion, Hartl's attempt to revive the performance of the so-called Innsbruck Easter Play (manuscript from 1391)[25] should be characterized as a completely fruitless endeavor. We do not know the place of performance. The play was not suited for the church, but rather for a marketplace or meadow. Was a stage put up, or did the event take place at ground level? Did the spectators stand before a scaffolding

23. "Aufführungen," p. 96.

24. See Albert B. Weiner, ed., *Philippe de Mézières' Description of the Festum praesentationis Beatae Mariae* (n.p., 1958).

25. Eduard Hartl, ed., *Das Drama des Mittelalters*, vol. 2, *Osterspiele* (Leipzig, 1937), pp. 122–35.

or did they surround the actors in a circle? The meager stage directions are mute on these points. From them, one can merely deduce that the *dramatis personae* mixed with the spectators. Hartl enumerates eight necessary stage locations in the following order: Hell, Synagogue, *unguentarius,* Pilate, apostles, Marys, grave, Heaven.[26] To be sure, his list lacks the ability to convince. He thinks in terms of a "stage," in any case, for he says that the *expositor ludi,* having spoken his words of introduction, remained standing, "probably at the edge of the stage," and "supervised" the play from there. The scene in Hell causes Hartl, as a "director," considerable discomfort. Hell had suffered a loss of souls through Christ's harrowing of it; in order to make good the loss, a distressed Lucifer convenes an assembly of devils, in that he "currit ad pallatium." Just what is this "pallatium" in relationship to Hell itself? Plainly a place, the location of which no longer can be determined, for the meeting of the infernal council. But such an answer does not satisfy Hartl. He expresses the suspicion that "pallatium" is a mocking reference to "dolium": "the barrel which, standing in the middle of the stage, is the customary seat of Lucifer in the great devil scenes." The "mocking" author —who, furthermore, practices his mockery only in Latin and, beyond that, only in a single rubric—is an invention of Hartl, who imported the vital barrel from Alsfeld.

From the epilogue, with which John takes farewell of the spectators, we can conclude that the performance had been supervised by members of the clergy ("dy pristere") and acted by pupils—by "armen schuler" (poor pupils), who were hungry and would be thankful for a reward in the form of a roast and pancakes.

Rolf Steinbach[27] has expressed his regret that the Innsbruck Easter Play is still not available in a satisfactory edition. The edition by Franz Joseph Mone was shot through with erroneous readings, and Hartl had "altered the text to meet the needs of a modern performance,"[28] using his text to produce the play several times with his Munich students.

THE RHENISH EASTER PLAY

Hans Rueff has tracked down the symbolic accents in forms of staging, and has coined the term "Bedeutungsbühne" in connection with his edition of the Rhenish Easter Play. His definition: "Dualisms of thought are expressed by symmetry of place."[29] He was thinking here of plays which "crystallized around the centers of

26. Ibid., p. 12.
27. *Die deutschen Oster- und Passionsspiele des Mittelalters* (Cologne, 1970), p. 63.
28. Ibid., p. 61.
29. *Das rheinische Osterspiel der Berliner Handschrift Ms. Germ. Fol. 1219, mit Untersuchungen zur Textgeschichte des deutschen Osterspiels* (Berlin, 1925), p. 46.

meaning of ecclesiastical celebrations, primarily without the intent of having the action produce the effect of an illusion"—thus they were centered around the grave and the manger. He made the subtle observation on the Rhenish Easter Play (ca. 1460): "In the middle there is the holy grave, the fact of the resurrection, which has its effect in two directions, opposed to one another. To the right of the sepulchre, the world of the faithful, to the left, the world of the adversaries. Play and counterplay. The action of the one never intrudes upon the scene of the other; the *monumentum* offers the sole connection between the two."[30]

Rueff has not treated the loca of the *Osterspiel* individually. The monumentum, at any rate, occupied the center, according to his concept. After all, the play begins with the "Resurrexi" of the resurrected Christ, dramatized by an accompanying mortar shot. If we follow Rueff's symbolic symmetry, we have on the one side the station of the apostles, a mansion with a table and benches for the meal of fish with the Savior. On the opposite side there is the place of assembly for *synagoga* and the four *milites*. Everything else is a hypothesis. In his sketch,[31] Walther Müller has placed Hell on the side of Christ's opponents. In addition, the rubrics require a location for the *medicus* and his servant, with a table on which the *servus* spreads out his wares. A table and chairs were needed for the Emmaus scene, probably on the Christian side. The question of a Paradise need not concern us, since Christ could simply lead the patriarchs, once they had been released from Limbo, off the "stage." Müller arrived at the conclusion that we are confronted here with a "sacral church stage, without naturalistic structures, sternly stylized." I cannot agree with Steinbach when he charges Müller with having erected "a kind of proscenium stage in the church."[32] When Müller quartered the medicus on the side of Christ's opponents, he anticipated a notion of Steinbach,[33] who interpreted the quack as a counterfigure to the Savior, the performer of miracles. In short: symbols *ad infinitum*.

THE PASSION I AND II IN THE "LUDUS COVENTRIAE"

The English cycle which we call the *Ludus Coventriae* (also the N.-Town Cycle or Hegge Plays) was never performed as a whole in the form in which it has been preserved. The manuscript is a compilation of three distinguishable play traditions. One group is comprised of plays on Old Testament material. The Marian plays provide

30. Ibid., p. 47.
31. *Der schauspielerische Stil*, p. 90.
32. *Die deutschen Oster- und Passionsspiele*, p. 95, n. 35.
33. Ibid., p. 97.

a second group, and the Passian play, in two parts, is a third segment, quite distinct from the other plays.[34] The episodes of the first and second group may have been presented in a processional fashion; the Passion play, however, did not trouble with pageant wagons, but rather was produced on some sort of stationary stage, with mansions set up more or less in a row—in a stage form, then, which is comparable to that of Valenciennes (1547).

The stage directions in the episodes from the Old Testament, and continuing as far as the awakening of Lazarus, are extremely terse, telling hardly anything about the appearance of the pageant wagons. Two examples: "Hic dormiunt reges et venit Angelus"—there is no indication of where the three kings are sleeping; and "Hic ascendit deus pinnaculum templi dum diabolus dicit," thus a raised place, about the appearance of which we are left uninformed.

As soon as we turn to the episodes which are included under the title "Passion Play I and II," the rubrics (which are now in English) have more of an illustrative air, and we can be sure that we are dealing with a polyscenic stage, on which the juxtaposed mansions and the actors are directed frontally toward the audience. I find no indications of a "performance in the round," postulated by Martial Rose,[35] or for "in-the-round staging of the type described by Richard Southern," proposed by Cameron and Kahrl. The expressions "place," "scaffold," and "stage" are not the exclusive possession of the theater-in-the-round; they are by no means "three theatrical terms identified with staging in the round," as Cameron and Kahrl assert.[36]

The majority of the mansions required for the Passion play can be identified. The high priest Annas, costumed as a bishop, is located "in his stage," in the company of two jurists and a messenger; he sends the latter to Caiaphas, who now reveals himself "in his skafhold." Caiaphas too has a brace of jurists with him. Annas has summoned Caiaphas to a council, which takes place at a third location, in a sort of chapel, "a lytil oratory," which is "in myd place" and is equipped with chairs. "Myd place" should not be defined as a center of a circle (on the Valenciennes frontispiece the palace stands "myd place"). After the conclusion of the Jews' council, Christ appears with his apostles. Two of the disciples fetch the ass on which Jesus "rydyth out of the place," that is, he leaves the platea and evidently remains invisible while Peter and

34. Kenneth Cameron and Stanley J. Kahrl, "The N-Town Plays at Lincoln," *Theatre Notebook* 20 (1965/66): 61–69.

35. In his edition, *The Wakefield Mystery Plays* (London, 1961), p. 39.

36. "Staging the N-Town Cycle," *Theatre Notebook* 21 (1967): 126. The authors envisage as a place of performance, at least for the Passion, the Lincoln Minster Close, though they also draw attention to a site called Broadgate, lying outside the city wall on the east, where a *Tobit* play was performed in 1566 and 1568.

John are preaching. Then the entrance into Jerusalem begins. Four citizens spread out their garments, children strew flowers and sing. Christ heals two blind men. He descends from his steed and laments the fate of Jerusalem.

The action now proceeds to the house of Simon Leprosus, in which Jesus eats the paschal lamb with his disciples. The meal remains a kind of *tableau vivant* for the time being, while the attention of the spectators turns once again to the oratory, the curtains of which are suddenly opened ("sodeynly onclose"). The council of the Jews, interrupted by the entrance of Jesus, continues, until the appearance of the penitent Mary Magdalene makes the audience look at Simon's house once again: here, Jesus forgives the sinful woman, Judas complains about the wasting of the spikenard, and Jesus predicts the betrayal. Judas gets up "and goth in the place" (i.e., into the neutral stage area), where he delivers his monologue before selling the Savior to the Jews. Meanwhile, the mansion of Simon is closed off by means of curtains. The council of the Jews now ends, and the high priests return to their scaffolds. The curtains of the mansion of Simon open ("sodeynly vn-close rownd Abowtyn") for the Last Supper and the washing of the feet.

Christ and his disciples now go to the Mount of Olives, which evidently was given the appearance of a little park ("a place lych to A park"). While the apostles are sleeping, an angel descends from Heaven to console the Savior ("An Aungel de-scendyth to jhesus and bryngyth to hym A chalys with An host ther in"). Jesus then goes with his disciples "in-to the place," where he is taken prisoner by Judas and the armed bailiffs. The Jews "lede cryst outh of the place." Mary Magdalene tells Mary the Mother what has happened. And so the first part ends.

A prologue of *Contemplacio* opens the second part. The speaker calls attention to the fact that a year has passed since the first part was performed. New mansions are required. In a procession the actors march "in to the place." Herod ascends his "schaf-falde." Pilate does the same. Annas and Caiaphas seem to share a house. A Hell is called for, too. The "house" of Pilate has a lady's chamber, in which the Devil appears to Pilate's wife. A "cowncel house" is attached to the mansion of Pilate, where Pilate sits in judgment and where the scourging and the crowning with thorns are enacted. A short scene at a crossroads follows, with Simon the Cyrenian and Veronica. The spatial relationship between Golgotha and the mansions remains obscure. The extensive rubrics end with the Crucifixion. They are scarcely noticeable in the remaining plays of the manuscript.

The responsibility for the performance of this Passion play was not borne by the guilds, whose religious zeal was fired by the great cycles of Chester and York. K. S. Block connected the Passion of the *Ludus Coventriae* with "a body of ecclesiastical actors."[37] In my opinion, this conjecture seems to hold water: both external and internal reasons appear to speak in its favor. First, let us approach the problem from without.

The manuscript comes from the third quarter of the fifteenth century. In the seventeenth century it was in the possession of Sir Robert Bruce Cotton, whose librarian, Richard James, gave the manuscript the title *Ludus Coventriae.* In this connection, James mentioned that these plays were given once upon a time by monks or brothers of a mendicant order ("actitata olim per monachos sive fratres mendicantes").[38] In his local history of Warwickshire, from 1656, W. Dugdale connected the religious plays in Coventry with the Feast of Corpus Christi, "which Pageants being acted with mighty state and reverence by the Friers of this House [the Franciscans]."[39] When Dr. Thomas Smith made the catalogue of the Cotton Collection in 1696, he removed the association with Coventry, but kept the reference to the mendicant order: "Videntur olim coram populo sive ad instruendum sive ad placendum a Fratribus mendicantibus representata."[40] In 1690 Humphrey Wanley gathered from the Coventry Annals that Henry VII had visited the city in 1493: "The King and Queen came to see the playes at ye greyfriers and much commended them."[41] Thomas Sharp investigated similar annals, noting the royal visit "to see the Plays acted by the Grey Friers."[42] In the word *at,* the majority of English scholars see a reference to the place from which the royal pair watched the plays; it was believed that this interpretation overcame the word *by* of Dugdale and Sharp, and, at the same time, did away with the notion that the Franciscans could have had a hand in the performance. The *per* and the *by* of the sources were easily dismissed.

Chambers grumbled about the Franciscan theory,[43] and wanted to get rid of the attribution of the plays to Coventry. Hardin Craig rejected the Franciscan thesis and the connection with Coventry, moving the site of the *Ludus* to Lincoln. He supported his action with linguistic peculiarities and with "the unequalled expansion of matters pertaining to the Blessed Virgin Mary,"[44] who was the object of special veneration in Lincoln. Of course, the cult of Mary may well connect the second group of plays with

37. K. S. Block, ed., *Ludus Coventriae, or the Plaie Called Corpus Christi,* Early English Text Society, e.s., 120 (London, 1922.) p. xxxiv.
38. Ibid., p. xxxvii.
39. Ibid., xxxviii.
40. Ibid.
41. Ibid., p. xl.
42. *Dissertation on the Pageants or Dramatic Mysteries, Anciently Performed at Coventry* (Coventry, 1825), p. 5.
43. *The Mediaeval Stage,* 2:420.
44. *English Religious Drama of the Middle Ages* (Oxford, 1955), p. 253.

Lincoln, but the Passion play itself has nothing more to do with the special veneration for Mary: it forms a group all to itself. For the rest, Craig has observed that the *Ludus* is much concerned with theological and moral themes, and Miss Block has made reference to the influence of Friar John's *Meditationes.*

At this point, I should like to direct attention to the internal (Franciscan) connections of the *Ludus* Passion with the Passion play of Alsfeld (1501). Rolf Steinbach called the Alsfeld Passion Play a "solemn sermon,"[45] a fusion of popular and didactic elements. On the frontispiece of the Alsfeld manuscript there is the entry: "S. Franciscus confessor domini, ora pro nobis omnibus." Thus we have an indication that the Franciscans had their hand in the "play," in some manner which cannot be made out at this juncture. The Alsfeld Passion emerged from the older Friedberg Passion (of which we possess only the director's register), and from Friedberg there is also a certain web of connections with the Villingen Passion, which was played in the garden of the Franciscan monastery at Villingen. Now the exchange of ideas among the members of a religious order is altogether conceivable. If it can be proved that theatrical performances were given under the aegis of the Franciscans in Friedberg, Alsfeld, and Villingen, could it not be true of their brothers in Coventry as well? In Friedberg and Alsfeld, moreover, performances were given "*per* and at" the Gray Friars. The "continental" stage form, which confronts us as something of a surprise in the Passion of the *Ludus,* could also find an explanation here.

The Alsfeld Passion has an allegorical figure in common with the *Ludus Coventriae:* Mors, a figure which otherwise does not customarily appear in Passion plays. In Alsfeld, Death appears twice: once as a mute figure ("si placet," thus at the pleasure of the director), walking past John the Baptist "lento pede," as John accepts the fate allotted him, and again—Mors has a speaking role this time—when he turns first to Lazarus and then to the public. The *Ludus Coventriae* also has a Mors scene, in the seventeenth *pagentum,* where he personally gives King Herod the quietus. The Alsfeld Mors, who comes to Lazarus, and the Mors of the *Ludus,* who puts an end to the life of Herod, show common features which I am inclined to regard not as accidental but as being rooted in the tradition of the Franciscan preachers.

In both plays we have a Death who introduces himself. If he says "death is my name"[46] in the *Ludus,* his Alsfeld counterpart begins with "Ich byn gnant der Toid" (v. 2155). Directly thereafter, in both instances, Mors boasts about his omnipotence: "All thynge that is on growd I welde at my wylle both man and beste."[47] And, in

---

45. *Die deutschen Oster- und Passionsspiele*, p. 164.
46. Block, *Ludus Coventriae* p. 174, v. 181.
47. Ibid., v. 182.

the same style: "nymmant kan sich vor mer verbergen, der ye gewan das leben uff erden" (vv. 2159–2160). And in both cases Mors holds a sermon against "hoffart" (v. 2192) or "preysyng of pride."[48] In both plays Death turns "ad populum" and reminds humankind of the vanity of all earthly things. In both plays he revels in the thought of physical decay: "Amonges wormys as I yow telle Vndyr the erth xul ye dwelle and thei xull Etyn both flesch and felle";[49] "dye wirm vorzerent das fleysch yn dem grabe" (v. 2190). If Mors sings his own praises in the *Ludus,* "wher I smyte ther is not grace,"[50] speaking threateningly of his "strokys," his "dentys," and his "spere," the Alsfeld Death serves up not only his "kulen," "barten," and "bogen," but the verse, "Alsus fellet uch des todes strigk" (v. 2185).

The relationship of the two addresses cannot be denied. It is not accidental. Here let me propose the hypothesis of a common origin, the sermonizing technique of the Franciscans, in order to support the relationship of the *Ludus Coventriae* to the Coventry Franciscans. Finally, we should remind ourselves that it was Saint Bonaventure who, in his *De reductione artium ad theologiam,* coined the phrase "theatrica autem est unica."

I am aware that linguistic features do not point to Coventry and that a number of researchers (Hardin Craig, Cameron and Kahrl) connect the *Ludus* with Lincoln. Alan H. Nelson[51] has a rather skeptical stance vis-à-vis the Lincoln hypothesis. In any event, the linguistic peculiarities are scarcely unambiguous. Moreover, I am not inclined to regard the dialect of the author (or perhaps of the several authors?) as in any way imposing a limitation upon the place of performance, particularly since the prologue (v. 527) eyes the possibility of performances in several towns (N.-Town?).

Claude Gauvin,[52] who has given us the most intensive analysis of the N.-Town Cycle which we thus far possess, is not wholly convinced that Lincoln was the place of performance, although she toys with the thought that the square before the cathedral was especially suited for it. To this the rejoinder may be made that the other English cycles could also be awakened to theatrical life on Lincoln's marvelous square. In her pursuit of a historical "dispositif," Miss Gauvin arrives at confusing conclusions. She divides the forty-one plays into five groups. A first group is comprised of Old Testa-

48. Ibid., v. 174.

49. Ibid., p. 177, vv. 281–83.

50. Ibid., p. 175, v. 190.

51. "Some Configurations of Staging in Medieval English Drama," in *Medieval English Drama,* ed. Jerome Taylor and Alan H. Nelson (Chicago, 1972), p. 131. Mark Eccles, *"Ludus Coventriae: Lincoln or Norfolk?," Medium Aevum,* 40 (1971): 140, likewise questions the Lincoln ascription and, on the basis of textual East Anglican characteristics, arrives at the conclusion that "the plays may have been acted in Norwich or in Lynn, or only on tour in more than one 'N.-town'."

52. *Un Cycle du théâtre religieux anglais du Moyen Âge. Le jeu de la ville de "N"* (Paris, 1973).

ment plays, a second of Marian plays. A third group includes the life of Christ from
the birth as far as the Passion, a fourth has the Passion I and II, and a fifth treats the
events after the Resurrection until Judgment Day. Gauvin's inquiry into forms of performance for the five groups results only in an insoluble dilemma, since she thinks in
terms of a "dispositif mobile" for the first group and a "dispositif fixe" for the Passion group. For the second group she imagines a transitional stage from "mobile" to
"fixe." The breaks in style, which arise quite naturally out of such a process, depend
upon Gauvin's concept that all five groups in the extant cycle were performed on a
certain feast day. The premise is an untenable one, since the groups owe their existence
to a variety of causes and to origins which we can no longer ascertain. They form a
"unity" only in the Codex Cotton Vespasian D.VIII in the British Museum. Gauvin
would like to place a "maître de la ville de N." at the side of the Wakefield Master
and the York Realist, a "maître" who is responsible not only for the two-part Passion
but who, as an "auteur-réviseur," put his stamp on the character of the whole cycle.
In her enthusiasm for the new "master," Claude Gauvin surely goes too far. This
cycle in particular shows no trace of a unifying hand.

Anne Cooper Gay[53] tars all the plays of the Hegge Cycle with the same brush, and
forces the Old Testament and Marian plays—which, beyond any doubt, belong to
another play tradition—into the stationary scheme of Passion I and II. Nelson shares
Miss Gay's opinion: "We may infer that the N.-Town cycle was always given a stationary production. Evidence for any use of pageant wagons is essentially nil. The
distinguishable parts of the cycle do not therefore reflect radically different methods of
stage production."[54]

Martial Rose, in his latest analysis of the Hegge Plays,[55] likewise views the N.-Town
Cycle as having been performed in its entirety after the "simultaneous mansions"
method. He is undecided, however, whether the spectators encircled the acting area or
fronted "a row or crescent of mansions (as in the Valenciennes Passion play illustra-
tions)." Rose offers us a choice: circular, semicircular, or frontal. But this marks progress over his original position (1961), which admitted only arena staging.

53. "The 'Stage' and the Staging of the N.-Town Plays," *Research Opportunities in Renaissance
Drama* 10 (1967): 135–40.

54. Nelson, "Some Configurations of Staging," p. 132.

55. "The Staging of the Hegge Plays," in *Medieval Drama,* ed. Neville Denny, Stratford-upon-
Avon Studies 16 (London, 1973): 197–221.

2   Topographical Evidence

THE PERFORMANCES to be discussed is this chapter can be localized—in cities, on squares, in certain churches. Stage plans, of the sort which we shall find in the next chapter, are not at our disposal, to be sure, but they may be partially divined, under favorable circumstances.

THE FRANKFURT PASSION (CA. 1450, 1493, 1498)

Julius Petersen, in his classic essay,[1] has deduced the manner of performance of the older Frankfurt Passion Play by employing the rubrics of the *Dirigierrolle* of Baldemar von Peterweil and by undertaking exemplary topographical detective work. His accomplishment, a model of its kind, does not require any corrections, although the proposal of Wolfgang F. Michael[2]—that the mansions of Petersen be placed in a central-perspective arrangement—is worth noting, since it would afford the audience beyond the ditch (*Graben*) a better view. Nevertheless, we should not exaggerate the importance of sight lines in the medieval theater.

No attempt has been made as yet to reconstruct the later Frankfurt Passion Play of 1493. Petersen himself uttered a warning against an application of his stage plan for the earlier play to the later one. To be sure, the so-called Samstagberg, the eastern part of the "Römer," may also be regarded as the place of performance of the 1493 play; yet architectonic changes had taken place there in the course of four decades, so that a stage plan for 1493 would have to proceed from altered topographical conditions.

More detailed information, assembled by R. Froning,[3] is available only for the play of 1498. Here, mention is made of a "machina," built with "ligna in magna copia," in other words, a stage platform, on which no less than 280 players performed. At that time, the Passion—the text of which is not preserved—was divided into four days. On June 4, Whitmonday, the story of Christ as far as the choosing of the Twelve was enacted, together with episodes from the Old Testament. On June 5 the performance concluded with the seizure of Christ, who then was dragged as a prisoner "per multas vicus civitatis." The next day the performance was begun with a similar

---

1. "Aufführungen."
2. *Frühformen der deutschen Bühne* (Berlin, 1963), p. 35.
3. R. Froning, ed., *Das Drama des Mittelalters,* Deutsche National-Litteratur 14 (Stuttgart, n.d.): 542–43.

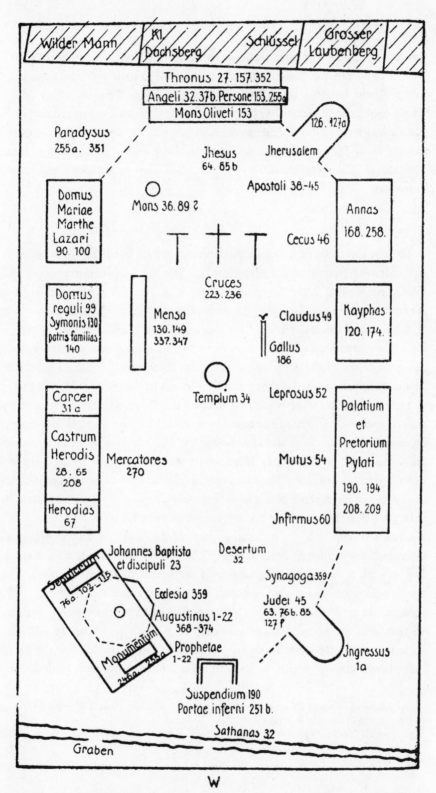

The older Frankfurt Passion Play (ca. 1450) on the Samstagberg, Frankfurt. Julius Petersen's reconstruction of the stage plan in his article, "Aufführungen und Bühnenplan des älteren Frankfurter Passionsspiels," *Zeitschrift für deutsches Altertum* 59 (1921/22): 122.

procession: Christ was once again led through the streets of Frankfurt, before the players assumed their positions on the "machina." On this day, the actor playing the role of Christ hung on the cross for almost two hours. The seventh of June was reserved for the Resurrection. The eighth of June witnessed a procession which led its participants through the Sachsenhausen gate, in order to erect the three crosses outside the city wall. The spiritual tension finally found a release in a banquet given for the participants. The vicar Johannes Kolmesser had been in charge of this series of performances.

MONS (1501)

The city can boast of a Passion performance which lasted for eight successive days, from Monday, July 5, to Monday, July 12. The place of performance was doubtless the Grand Marché in the center of the city. Gustave Cohen made an important discovery when, in 1913, he found the promptbook of the meneur de jeu in the archives of the Mons Municipal Library.[4] In addition, Cohen published the expense accounts for the performances, which contain exact figures of the "depenses de la Passion." In his introduction to the *Livre de conduite,* the French scholar attempted a reconstruction of the performance, without getting very far in the process. He gave us glimpses of certain "backstage" activities; he illuminated the mechanics of several *trucs* and *secretz,* and made a minute examination of both Heaven and Hell. But even this rich documentation, almost as abundant as for the Lucerne Play of 1583, does not permit an unequivocal reconstruction. What would we do in Lucerne's case if we lacked the two stage plans of Cysat? For Mons we simply have no stage plan at all. According to Cohen's count, seventy places of action (*lieux,* or mansions) were needed in Mons; to be sure, the scholar did not know where to put them. Cohen was of the opinion that Heaven and Hell were the two corner-posts of the stage, the dimensions of which he estimated at seventy by twenty meters.[5] There is no question that the stage (*hourd*) had its back against the southeast side of the houses of the marketplace. The stands for the spectators (*parq*) lay opposite, in the direction of the Hotel de Ville. In the "compte de depenses" Cohen found a mention of two houses which had some connection with the hourd, the "maison dite de la Seuwe," where the entrance to the stage was obviously located, and the "maison d'Allemaigne," where the deluge scene was played, a scene which, in its turn, had a close connection with the Heavenly

---

4. *Le livre de conduite du régisseur et le compte des dépenses pour le Mystère de la Passion joué à Mons en 1501* (Strasbourg, 1925).

5. *Études d'histoire du théâtre en France au Moyen-Age et à la Renaissance* (Paris, 1956), p. 234.

Paradise. When, bearing this information in mind, one looks at the situation on the map of the marketplace which Cohen has provided, one is inclined to allot a central position to Paradise, and thus not a position at a corner-post.

There is still work to be done here, even though—in the absence of an authentic stage plan—a universally satisfactory solution might never be reached. The most pressing task, and something which Cohen neglected, would be the division of the cycle into performance days, or, more precisely, half-days, since the performance took place during the morning and, after a midday break, during the afternoon for eight days hand running. Such an investigation would show that the stage setting changed from day to day in accordance with the exigencies of the play.

ROMANS (1509)

The town had three patron saints, Séverin, Félicien, and Exupère, whose relics were revered by its inhabitants. When Romans suffered a great drought in 1504, the relics of the martyrs were carried through the streets in a procession, while the populace prayed for rain. The next day it rained, and the citizens decided to express their gratitude to the three saints by giving a *mystère*.

The performances of this *Mystère des trois Doms* took place at Whitsuntide in 1508, on May 27, 28, and 29, both in the morning and the afternoon. The place of performance was the garden of the Franciscan monastery ("Cour des Cordeliers") of Saint Bernard. With its roughly 10,000 verses, the play made great demands, of a technical nature above all. Actors had to be found for 96 roles; in addition, there were numerous extras.

Basing his work on the account books which he had discovered, Paul-Emile Giraud[6] published various details about the ambitious undertaking. The text was not found by Giraud until the beginning of the 1880s; after his death, it was published by Ulysse Chevalier, with additional information from the archives.[7] Thus we have the following material: the text with extensive rubrics, the list of participants, information about rehearsals, and exact accounts of expenditures and receipts. We even know what colors the painter François Tévenot used. In addition, the dimensions of the stage and the space for the spectators are known. Once again, we possess relatively rich documentation, but—alas!—no plan of the stage. The temptation to make a diagram is strong.

The interesting performance was more or less ignored by French scholarship. Cohen

---

6. *Composition, mise en scène et représentation du mystère des Trois Doms* (Lyon, 1848).
7. Paul-Emile Giraud and Ulysse Chevalier, *Le mystère des Trois Doms* (Lyon, 1887).

evidently found the available material to be unimportant, compared with his dis-
coveries in Mons. Grace Frank has given this mystère no attention whatsoever. To my
knowledge, only one attempt at a reconstruction was published, by Glynne Wickham,[8]
in a postscript to the eighth chapter of his book about the English stage. In my seminar, students have examined the topic several times, and in doing so have come to
conclusions which, in part, do not agree with Wickham's stage plan.

A document important for any reconstruction is a "Notice" of Louis Perrier, a judge
in Romans, who left a brief eyewitness account of the performance. His testimony is
significant insofar as he was partially responsible for the performance's being held,
and in that he undertook to act a role of considerable importance in the play. It is
through Perrier that we learn the dimensions of the stage and certain details about its
decorations. According to his account, the platform was "trente six pas de long et xviij
de large."[9] At the four corners of the rectangular stage there were four towers, painted
gray. The platform was four feet high and surrounded by a balustrade adorned with
foliage or flowers. A curtain kept the section beneath the stage, which had been deep-
ened by means of excavations, from the view of the spectators. On the stage there
stood "tres excellantz chaffaulx," Paradise in the east, Hell in the west. Between these
poles were the mansions for the play's events, which took place in Rome, Vienne,
Lyons, and elsewhere. "Tous les jours change la station cellon le mistere."[10]

The spectators sat on wooden stands that rose upward like an amphitheater and
were surmounted by a row of loges, eighty-four "chambres." As a protection against
rain, canopies had been stretched above the spectators and the stage, a wise precaution,
for it rained before and after the performance on each of the three days. In addition,
the space for the spectators had a depth of six *toises,* that is, of about twelve meters.
The garden of the Franciscan monastery is plainly visible on an old map of Romans;
even three of the elms, whose branches had to be trimmed, are registered there.

Thus far we are on safe ground. We have Paradise in the east, Hell in the west, and
four corner towers, of which one serves as a prison while the other three symbolized
the continents of Asia, Africa, and Europe. We find ourselves uncertain as soon as we
try to make a sketch for the location of the towers and mansions. Wickham's plan
gives the impression that the arrangement of the mansions—an arbitrary one, it must
be added—was the same on all three days of performance. But this was by no means
the case. "Lyon" was needed only on the first and third days of the performances. Be-

8. *Early English Stages, 1300–1660* (London and New York, 1959), 1:306.
9. The final dimensions of the stage were larger than originally planned: *"la placta forma plus
granda,"* Giraud/Chevalier, *Mystère des Trois Doms,* p. 631.
10. Ibid., p. 592.

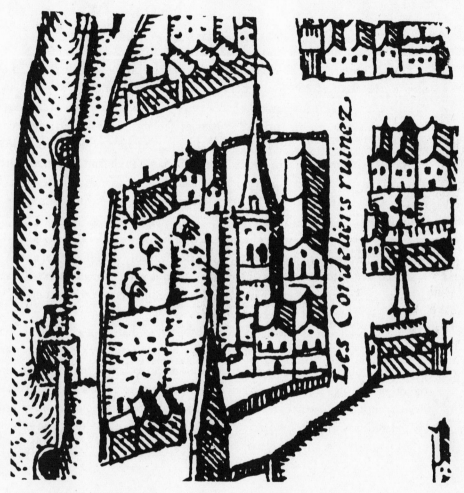

The courtyard of the Franciscan monastery at Romans, site of the 1509 performance of the *Mystère des trois Doms*. Detail of a map completed around 1612.

sides, the first day required a space for "Mt. Senis" and a house for the pope. Here the guesswork begins, supported only imperfectly by the rubrics and by internal evidence, so that various scholars would arrive at various conclusions, should they undertake to determine whether "Rome" was placed on the side of Hell and "Vienne" in the east, or vice versa.

BOURGES (1536)

The performance of the *Actes des Apôtres* of the brothers Greban, which contributed to the fame of the city of Bourges and its textile industry, was introduced on April 30, 1536, by a procession of the dramatis personae in their costumes. An account of this *monstre* has survived.[11] Jacques Thiboust is commonly regarded as the description's author,[12] a well-to-do merchant who, describing the costumes used in the performance of the *Actes,* proceeded with justifiable pride and the utmost precision. Thus we have been acquainted with the flamboyant costumes for the roughly 700 participants (494 speaking roles) ever since the publication of the monstre manuscript in 1836.

Two pageant wagons were also included in the monstre, a Hell wagon at the beginning of the procession and a wagon for the Heavenly Paradise at the end. Thiboust —for we shall call our anonymous reporter by this name—gives an exact description of these wagons. At the moment, we shall not come to a decision concerning their possible use as mansions during the performance.

There is no doubt about the location of the performance. Jean Chaumeau[13] stated that the performance of the *Actes* took place in the "fosse des arenes." The "sandpit" is plainly visible on a map of Bourges published in 1567. Opinions are divided as to the origin of this "fosse." Chaumeau speaks of the remains of an amphitheater from Roman antiquity. The chronicler of the journey of the Barons von Zimmern calls it a "wundergrossen gruben," where a "grose thurn" stood at one time—in other words, a fortification.[14] At any rate, Passion plays had taken place in this "pit" since 1497.[15]

---

11. [Jacques Thiboust], *La relation de l'ordre de la triomphante et magnifique monstre du Mystère des Actes des Apôtres faite à Bourges* (Bourges, 1836).

12. Raymond Lebègue, *Le Mystère des Actes des Apôtres* (Paris, 1929), p. 90, was inclined to question Thiboust's authorship, but did not come up with an alternative suggestion.

13. *Histoire de Berry* (Lyons, 1566), p. 238.

14. K. Christ, "Die Aufführung von Mysterien in Issoudun (1535) und Bourges (1536) nach dem Bericht der Zimmerischen Chronik," *Zeitschrift für französische Sprache und Litteratur* 46 (1923): 319.

15. Lebègue, *Mystère des Actes des Apôtres,* p. 78.

Chaumeau attended a Passion play lasting several days, which was given before 25,000 to 30,000 spectators.[16]

According to the German chronicler, an "amphitheatro" had been prepared for the *Actes* which in its dimensions almost rivaled the Roman Colosseum. The reference to the Colosseum can only be interpreted to mean that the stands for the spectators surrounded the arena in a circle or oval, and the play took place in the "pit." The German chronicler did not see the play himself, but witnessed the preparations. Chaumeau speaks of an "amphithéâtre" too, and he was a learned man, who had read his Elder Pliny and referred to the amphitheater erected by C. Curio. Thus, speaking of an amphitheater in Bourges, Chaumeau meant an amphitheater in the antique sense of the word. And so we are confronted with a circular theater, just as we have evidence of a similar form for a performance of the *Actes* at Paris in 1541. (Neil C. Brooks[17] brought the interesting Parisian document to the light of day.) The decisive passage of the journal entry runs as follows: "vnd was dat Theatrum gemaicht int Ronde off die Romische alde maniere, dat alle menschen sitten mochten, die eyn hoeger dan di ander. . . ."

According to Chaumeau the *cavea* in Bourges consisted of "degrez," that is, benches ascending in the manner of an amphitheater and topped by a two-story gallery (loges?): "Ledict Amphitheâtre estoit à deux etaiges surpassans la sommité des degrez."[18] An awning of various colors was stretched over the whole stadium.

James Hashim[19] rejected the theory of a circular theater, thinking instead of an arrangement for the auditorium and stage in a pseudo-Vitruvian style, in which the mansions, drawn up in a row, would have formed a kind of *scaenae frons*. He allocated a quarter of the circle for the stage, while the auditorium occupied about three-fourths of the circle.

Now let us turn our attention to another primary source, a manuscript in the Bourges library containing a list of the persons appearing in the *Actes* (including an account of the number of verses they had to speak) and an "Extraict des Fainctes."[20] The "Extraict" provides information concerning the mansions needed for the cycle, although nothing is revealed about their appearance. The "Extraict" also includes particulars about the special effects, which the *Actes* required in rich measure. The

16. Ibid., p. 79.

17. "Notes on Performances of French Mystery Plays," *Modern Language Notes* 39 (1924): 280.

18. *Histoire de Berry*, p. 237.

19. "Notes towards a Reconstruction of *Le Mystère des Actes des Apôtres* as Presented at Bourges, 1536," *Theatre Research* 12 (1972): 42.

20. The documents were published by A. de Girardot, *Mystère des Actes des Apôtres représenté à Bourges en avril 1536.* (Paris, 1854).

technical secrets, to be sure, are not betrayed. In any event, these documents are no substitute for a *Livre de conduite,* such as is available in the case of Mons.

Thus far we are supported by tolerably certain facts. They are not sufficient, of course, to allow a reconstruction of the performance; a plethora of uncertainties stands in the way of such an undertaking. In the first place, an exact text is lacking. In the editio princeps, which Guillaume Alabat published two years after the performance, sections have been removed which could have aroused the displeasure of Protestant readers. Such passages were not withheld from the theater public, which was over-whelmingly Catholic.[21] The two manuscript versions cannot be regarded as prompt copies. In short, we can come fairly close to the text as it was performed, but absolute authenticity (as, for example, is guaranteed in the case of Lucerne) cannot be expected here.

The next question is, when did the performances take place? Up to the present, an answer satisfactory to all scholars has still not been reached. Only the date of the monstre is certain, April 30. The statement that the performances lasted (or took?) forty days comes from Chaumeau. If we read Chaumeau as meaning that there were daily performances, the last of these would have taken place on June 8. Since the cycle included about 60,000 verses, only about 1,500 would have been recited daily. Spectators would scarcely have taken the trouble of following such subdivisions. Or were there perhaps performances only on the Sundays and holidays within the forty-day term? In his *Histoire de Berry* (1689), La Thaumassière reported that the performances ended on June 14. Further confusion is caused by an entry in the books of the Cathedral of Saint-Etienne to the effect that a performance had taken place as late as August 3. Finally, there exists a diary entry of the notary Delacroix,[22] according to which the performances lasted into October.

The making of a stage plan would be a hopeless undertaking. Having clouded his own view by means of his idea of a scaenae frons, Hashim has voiced a few conjectures about the grouping of the loca on the basis of the rather complete list of mansions—conjectures which belong, in fact, to the realm of the imagination. Furthermore, he has expressed the opinion that the pageant wagons shown in the monstre—Heaven and Hell—also served as mansions during the performance. I cannot agree. The pageant wagon for Paradise was nothing more than a very decorative pageant wagon. In contrast, the Paradise mansion required for the play was elevated, and fitted out with equipment for flying machines. The pageant wagon, with its dimensions of eight

21. See Lebègue, *Mystère des Actes des Apôtres,* pp. 35–73.
22. Quoted in ibid., p. 101.

by twelve feet, could not meet the demands of the play. The same may be said of the Hell wagon (eight by fourteen feet), which simply would not have been functional as a Hell mansion. After all, the affluent citizens of Bourges could afford to order two special pageant wagons for the monstre alone.

It may safely be assumed that the Bourges stage had an extended network of traps and subterranean passageways: again and again, saints and devils, tigers and dogs disappear and reappear "par soubz terre." Thus we (in opposition to Lebègue) may think of a raised platform stage, under which all the subterranean traffic could flow without a hitch. The German chronicler reports that the theater had an installation by which water could be conducted into the stage space. This justifies us in assuming that the sea scenes called for in the manuscript were in fact enacted with real water.

FLORENCE (1439)

Two remarkable Florentine religious performances, which Bishop Abraham of Ssusdal witnessed in 1439, are identified with two churches: the Play of the Annunciation with the Church of the Santissima Annunziata and the Play of the Ascension with Santa Maria del Carmine. The Russian bishop described the performances with the greatest clarity, even noting technical details. Ssusdal's eyewitness report[23] is a unique document, a source without parallel in the history of the medieval theater. It would not be difficult to reconstruct these productions.

For the performance of an Annunciation play in the S. Felice church, Filippo Brunelleschi had discovered other technical solutions, on which Vasari bestowed approval in his *Vita*. We are indebted to James Watrous for a rendering of Filippo's *apparato;* Orville K. Larson has published it.[24]

BESANÇON, MAGDEBURG, SION

Dunbar H. Ogden[25] has made an attempt to localize performances of liturgical dramas on appropriate church plans. In all likelihood, the Church of Saint John the Evangelist in Besançon, with its two apses, one on the east, the other on the west, was employed for the *Visitatio Sepulchri* and the *Officium Stellae* in the manner deduced by Ogden. In a similar fashion, Ogden has superimposed the Magdeburg *Visitatio*

23. In a German translation by Alexander Wesselofsky, "Italienische Mysterien in einem russischen Reisebericht des XV. Jahrhunderts," *Russische Revue* 10 (1877): 425–41.

24. "Vasari's Descriptions of Stage Machinery," *Educational Theatre Journal* 9 (1957): 287–99.

25. "The Use of Architectural Space in Medieval Music-Drama," *Comparative Drama* 8 (1974): 63–76.

onto the ground plan of that city's cathedral. Here, however, the "stage directions" are quite vague, so that the Magdeburg experiment appears less satisfying.

The line of march in the Fleury *Coming of the Magi* was sketched by Wolfgang F. Michael[26] onto the plan of the abbey church of Fleury, although Michael was aware that Fleury cannot be regarded as the play's place of origin. Naturally, objections can be made to such a procedure. Michael is on far more solid ground when he encloses the Sion Magi Play in that town's Church of Notre-Dame-de-Valère,[27] and solves the problem of the rood-screen by moving the "main action" into the choir itself. However, I do not believe that an "audience" was present: I regard this play of the Three Wise Men as a liturgical celebration, intended for the clergy.

TEGERNSEE (TWELFTH CENTURY)

Michael, furthermore, has lodged the Tegernsee *Ludus de Antichristo* in an imaginary church.[28] The rubrics make no reference to a church interior, yet the ceremonial style of the *Ludus* suggests a church's interior. Chambers advanced his opinion: "It [the *Ludus*] must have taken up the whole nave of some great church."[29] The extensive rubrics apportion the requisite sedes to three points of the compass. Michael places the Temple of the Lord in the choir, near the main altar. He locates the emperor, as well as the French and German kings, at the west end of the nave. The remaining sedes are then accommodated in the side aisle to the south. Only the north side aisle is left for the spectators; from here they could not see the happenings at the west end of the church and could scarcely hear them. Stylistic factors make us think of a performance inside a church. Only secondary importance need be given the pamphlet (1161) of Gerhoh von Reichersberg, who thundered against church performances, crying bloody murder at an Antichrist play (which has disappeared). The location of the various sedes will not be ascertained with any finality in the future, either. Despite the presence of battle scenes, the arrangement of the loca could be carried out under more limited conditions of space than Michael has provided for: he laid claim to the whole church. I incline toward the assumption that the spectators, wherever they may have had their seats, were members of the clergy and the local nobility. It would have made little sense to produce this spiritualized piece of knightly poetry before spectators who understood neither the language nor the meaning of the play.

We have no evidence that the *Ludus* was performed before the church at Tegernsee,

26. *Frühformen der deutschen Bühne*, p. 20.
27. Ibid., p. 14.
28. Ibid., pp. 24–25.
29. *The Mediaeval Stage*, 2:63.

as Borcherdt assumed. Kindermann entertains a similar notion: it was performed "with great pomp before the abbey church in Tegernsee."[30] We can only agree with Karl Young here: "It is a pleasant but idle fancy that the background of the platea may have been, on one or more occasions, one of the portals of the church at Tegernsee itself."[31]

THE EASTER PLAY OF TOURS

Cohen's reconstruction of a church performance, an attempt made with the *Ludus Paschalis* of Tours, may appropriately be discussed here: he arrived at some quite bizarre conclusions.[32]

His place of performance is, again, an ideal church with a narthex. In the course of the play, Mary Magdalene, "in sinistra parte ecclesia stans," sings her aria of lament. This allows us to assume that the performance took place in a church, and Cohen indicated the location for Mary Magdalene on the left side of his church plan, at the junction of the choir and the transept. The scholar assumed that the high altar was used as the grave of Christ, a proposal to which an objection can scarcely be raised.

The problem arises (for Cohen, at any rate) with the rubric preceding the entrance of the three Marys: "Tunc veniant ante hostium ecclesie et di[cant]." The "ante hostium" misled Cohen into locating the introductory scenes before the portal of the church; he proceeded under the assumption that the faithful gathered in front of the narthex, in order to watch the beginning of the play. Here—in other words, before the church—Pilate gives his soldiers the task of guarding the grave. Singing, the soldiers then march into the church to a point in front of the high altar, or *sepulchrum*. No sooner have they arrived than they are cast to the ground by an angel's lightning bolt; they will not stand up again until after the visitatio, when the report is made to Pilate. It is impossible to understand how Cohen could arrive at the assumption that the striking effect with the angel and his lightning bolt took place in a church which was still empty, while the spectators were still standing in front of the church, where they would watch the scene with the unguentarius. They would crowd into the church, where the rest of the scenes took place, only when the three Marys entered. Here Cohen dreamed of a "mouvement processionel,"[33] of the kind which Maeterlinck once

30. Heinz Kindermann, *Theatergeschichte Europas* (Salzburg, 1957), 1:271.
31. *The Drama of the Medieval Church*, 2:395.
32. Gustave Cohen, *Anthologie du drame liturgique en France au Moyen-Age* (Paris, 1955), pp. 36–37. Eduard Krieg, *Das lateinische Osterspiel von Tours* (Würzburg, 1956), does not deal with production problems.
33. Cohen, *Anthologie du drame liturgique,* p. 37.

envisioned for his production of *Hamlet*. In this case, Pilate must have followed the Marys, too, for he, after all, also had a station in the church since the sentinels had to report the Resurrection to him. A totally untenable reconstruction, which can be traced, simply, to a misunderstanding of "ante hostium." Karl Young[34] has a more correct interpretation on this point: the "ante hostium" is to be understood in the sense that the Marys, having finished their entrance through the church portal, immediately began to sing as they walked through the main aisle to the sepulchrum. The spectators had long since foregathered in the church.[35]

Cohen attempted to distribute the remaining stations in the church itself. For the *hortulanus* scene he chose the left side of the choir, and decided to place the station for the apostles on the right side of the altar. Pilate received the report of the sentinels on the right side, directly opposite the position of Mary Magdalene. These, of course, are nothing but unproved and unprovable hypotheses. As a matter of fact, we only know that Magdalene gave vent to her despair "in sinistra parte," and that the Marys entered through a door—in short, we seem to know very little.

34. *The Drama of the Medieval Church*, 1:449–50.
35. Chambers, *The Mediaeval Stage*, 2:39, n. 2, also thought of a performance within a church: "But *'ante'* may be inside."

3 Stage Plans

EQUIPPED with a text, its rubrics, and some topographical material from the archives, we were but rarely in the position of being able to achieve even approximate certainty about the performance conditions of the plays mentioned thus far. Now, official stage plans are added to our equipment, and, thanks to the information imparted by them, we shall be spared a good many foggy hypotheses.

LUCERNE (1583)

There is no need for guesswork here. An exemplary edition of the text was published by Heinz Wyss.[1] We have been given access to Renward Cysat's memoranda, his "Abtheilung der Plätzen" and his "Denkrodel der Kleydung," by M. Blakemore Evans.[2] The two stage plans sketched by Cysat (day one and day two) have long been known to scholarship. The extant documents leave hardly a single question unanswered. An authentic replica of the 1583 production could be staged on the Weinmarkt tomorrow, as a tourist attraction.

Hans Rueff characterized Cysat's stage plan as an attempt "to reproduce the natural scene of the action topographically"; "without giving a thought to style," Cysat relinquished "the practical utilization of the space to the director."[3] But at the same time Rueff had to admit that the scenic arrangement was thoroughly suited to the style of the *Osterspiel*: "The action of the play was expansive, relaxed, episode followed loosely on episode without any inner necessity for the succession of events, without any attempt to work out a gradual intensification in the plan."[4] The use of "Wechselbühnen" was denoted by Rueff as being characteristic for Lucerne. He detected in the plan only two fixed poles which were not subject to this "Wechsel," or change—Heaven and Hell. He overlooked the fact that the Temple also kept its identity throughout the two days of the performance. I believe, moreover, that the term "Wechselbühne" is not appropriate for Lucerne. Rueff used it to mean that there were mansions which changed their function in the course of the play. We come across an example of this practice in Valenciennes, where "la salle" had its function changed in accordance with the different localities it represented. In Lucerne, only the Garden of

1. *Das Luzerner Osterspiel*, 3 vols. (Bern, 1967).
2. *The Passion Play of Lucerne* (New York, 1943).
3. *Das rheinische Osterspiel*, p. 43.
4. Ibid., p. 44.

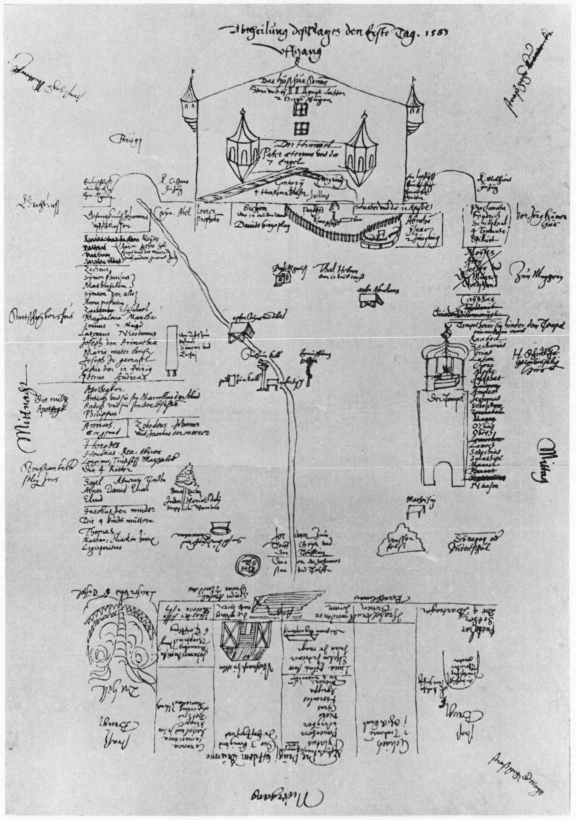

Renward Cysat's stage plan for the first day of the *Osterspiel* production of 1583 on the Fischmarkt in Lucerne. Original in the Zentralbibliothek, Lucerne.

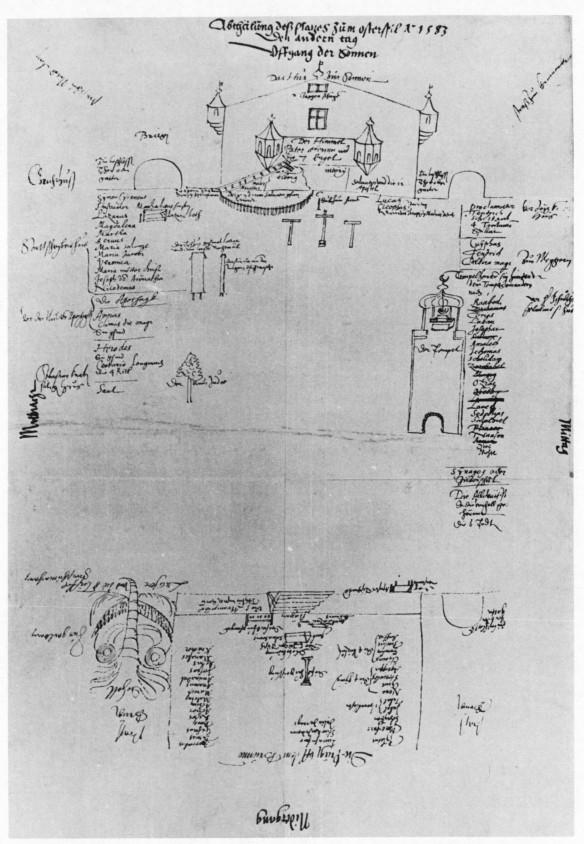

Cysat's arrangement of the mansions and stations on the second day. Zentralbibliothek. Lucerne

Eden was redefined in Rueff's sense: on the second day it served as the Garden of Gethsemane. Yet even in this case, a shift was made from the right to the left. Other loca, needed only on the first day, were not employed again on the second: the Christmas hut was not given a new task; it was replaced by the whipping post and some traps which served as graves. The little mansion which had been required for the Annunciation scene was not put to another use. Insofar as possible, the holding positions of the actors remained the same for the two days. The Christian party awaited the cues of the *regens ludi* in front of the city clerk's house on both days. The vendor of ointments always stood before the apothecary's house.

ALSFELD (1501)

Performances of the Passion can be authenticated for the years 1501, 1511, and 1517—expanded in 1511, abbreviated in 1517, when the play had to be broken off early because of rain. The Passion was intended for performance on three days; around 3,000 verses were recited daily. We know nothing about the place of the performance. Dörrer leaned toward "a space before the church or the town hall."[5]

On the last page of the manuscript there is a stage plan, which R. Froning attempted to interpret.[6] If we read the sketch according to the needle of his compass, we have "Thronus" in the south—the Heavenly Paradise, beyond any question. In front of it are three crosses. In the extreme north there is a place called "Ortus," probably the Mount of Olives. In the west we find four "castra." Reading in a north-south direction counterclockwise, we discover first the "castrum Herodis"; adjacent to it, "Secundum patris familias et reguli"; then "Tertium Pilati"; and finally "Marthe cum suis." The four mansions are arranged like houses along a street. Across this "street" five more mansions are lined up beside one another: Annas in the north, then Jerusalem, Synagogue, Caiaphas, and finally Nicodemus and Joseph of Arimathea. In the southwestern corner there is the notation "Desertum Johannis disponatur ad placitum." The plan does not provide a place for Hell.

Publishing a schematic reproduction of the stage plan, Michael[7] reproached Froning for having entered the "Ortus" into the upper middle part of his plan.[8] The "Ortus," according to Michael,[9] was "in fact on the upper right side," thus above the

5. Anton Dörrer in *Die deutsche Literatur des Mittelalters, Verfasserlexikon*, ed. Wolfgang Stammler and Karl Langosch (Berlin, 1953), vol. 3, col. 721.
6. Froning, *Das Drama des Mittelalters*, p. 267.
7. *Frühformen der deutschen Bühne*, p. 36.
8. Froning, *Das Drama des Mittelalters*, p. 860.
9. *Frühformen der deutschen Bühne*, p. 162, n. 27.

Stage plan for the Alsfeld Passion Play (1501). Original in the Landesbibliothek, Kassel.

mansion of Annas. A glance at the original plan will show, however, that Froning's positioning of the Garden was correct: the "Ortus" lies "ex opposito" to the cross of the Savior. Michael's thesis—"One side is left open, obviously for the spectators"[10]—thus collapses. I am not convinced that, in Alsfeld, we are confronted with an arrangement similar to that which Petersen inferred from the Frankfurt Dirigierrolle. Studying the rubrics, I get the feeling, on the contrary, that here, for once, we may postulate a circular arrangement of the mansions and of the public as well. The stage directions provide definite indications of such an arrangement. The Proclamator begins his address "in medio ludi." He calls the spectators' attention to the fact that "wer da betredden wirt in dissem kreyss" will be taken to Hell by the devils, no matter who he may be, if he "nit gehoret in dit spiel." And when the Proclamator finally gives the command to the chief magistrate, "macht ir den slagk," the official may have closed a barrier which prevented entrance into the area of the stage action. Later, a barrel ("doleum") is employed, "quod positum est in medio ludi"; it served as the pinnacle of the Temple. After her conversion, Magdalene tells of the transformation in a monologue which she has to deliver "circumeundo circulum." The blind man and his servant begin to sing and must "transire versus sinistrum manum circuli," in order to meet the Savior. Thus there is constant reference to a circular form.

As mentioned above, there is no space set aside for Hell on the plan. From the rubrics we learn that Hell was a large barrel, which had a door that could be closed and a window. Lucifer climbs onto this barrel ("ascendit doleum") to make his address to the devils. It would be senseless to undertake any conjectures concerning the location of Hell. Christ might possibly have had his point of departure beneath the "Thronus." The assembled disciples also received the Holy Spirit there. Steps led up to the elevated "Thronus" ("Duo angeli in scala canunt"). From the stage directions we can also conclude that the "castrum" of Herod was of considerable size and solidity: the king celebrated his birthday with a banquet; the daughter of Herodias danced; Herodias had her own sedes, where she was visited by Satan; a soldier stood on the roof of the mansion and then descended, to dance with the worldly Magdalene.

Despite all this information, a reconstruction of the performance would be extremely speculative and, on that account, meaningless. Nor has an attempt in this direction been made, thus far. In the case of Alsfeld, we receive no help from the director's prompt copy, discovered in 1891[11]; since we cannot make a precise deter-

10. Ibid., p. 35.
11. Hans Legband, "Die Alsfelder Dirigierrolle," *Archiv für hessische Geschichte und Altertums-kunde,* n. s., 3 (1904): 393–456.

mination of the place of performance, the Petersen method, so fruitful for Frankfurt, is not applicable here. Nevertheless, we understand from the director's register, intended for the 1511 performance, that the text of the play was "of a flexible structure" (Legband's phrase) and that, over against the play's manuscript, some cuts and some additions were provided. While John spoke his memento mori, not only Mors but also Tempus appeared. The allegorical figure of Time had also, at the end of the first and second days, to deliver a "rigmum," the text of which is not preserved.

Rueff numbers the Alsfeld sketch among those stage plans which bring to view "an inner order of the action." He discovered a principle of organization in the stage plan: "The persons with a close inner relationship to the Savior have their positions not far from His place beneath the 'Thronus'. The opponents, sharply divided into the matching forces of worldly and spiritual power, move away from the side of Heaven. The position of the crypto-Christians, Nicodemus and Joseph, looks almost like an over-subtle solution of a difficult problem: they stand beside Christ and opposite the house which the faithful frequent, and yet they form a wing of the Jewish party."[12]

DONAUESCHINGEN (ca. 1485)

We possess the text with quite exact stage directions and, on the first page of the manuscript, a list of the "hüsser vnd höff" needed in the two-day play. Six leaves are missing at the end of the manuscript, and with them the list of costumes. The stage plan accompanying the manuscript caused confusion until it was recognized that it would not serve for the Donaueschingen Passion. (We shall say more about this matter in the section on Villingen.)

Among the loca enumerated in the introductory rubric, one mansion deserves particular attention: "ein gemeine burge, dar in man kront, geislet, das nachtmal vnd ander ding volbringt." In other words, we are confronted here with an essentially neutral mansion, which has its function changed several times and which could be described with the expression coined by Rueff, "Wechselbühne."[13] It is strange that the official list of loca ignores Christ's sepulchre. Was "Lausarus grab" to be used again for this purpose?

The attempt to draw a stage plan with the help of the list of mansions and the rubrics would be doomed to failure from the start. Walther Müller's optimism is not justified: "In its particulars, the stage plan can easily be reconstructed by reference to

12. Rueff, *Das rheinische Osterspiel,* pp. 45–46.
13. Ibid., p. 43.

the stage structures—about 18 of them are required."[14] In our discussion of Villingen, we shall have the opportunity to see to what phantasms such efforts (made by Chambers, Evans, Hartl, Rapp, and Rueff) have led.[15]

VILLINGEN (ca. 1585)

Manuscript 137 of the Fürstlich Fürstenbergische Hofbibliothek in Donaueschingen contains the text, from around 1485, of the Donaueschingen Passion Play. F. J. Mone,[16] the first editor of this play, found the drawing of a stage plan on a loose sheet which was enclosed with the paper manuscript; it has long been regarded as the stage plan of the Donaueschingen Passion Play.

The same Donaueschingen library possesses a second Passion-play manuscript, bearing the number 138. It contains the Villingen Passion Play, which is younger than the Donaueschingen play by about one hundred years. The prologue of the Villingen Passion Play mentions the foundation of a "Bruoderschafft" in Villingen in 1585. The association undertook the task of producing the two-part Villingen Passion. The bindings of the manuscript bear the date 1600. The text shows signs of various revisions and so might well have been used for performances between 1585 and 1600. The Villingen Passion Play has many features in common with the Donaueschingen play, often repeating it word for word; but there are also certain differences, to which attention will be called below: in this process, to be sure, I have had to keep to the facts preesnted by Dinges[17] and Roder,[18] since the text of the Villingen Passion was not accessible to me.

The manuscript of the Villingen Passion Play once belonged to the Franciscans in Villingen, and the performances of the play may have owed their birth and their continued existence to the initiative of the Franciscans. At any rate, it was the Franciscans who brought about the performance of the *Tragicomoedia passionis Dominicae* in Villingen on March 21 and 29, 1646.[19] Roder has determined that there were earlier performances of the Passion play in Villingen, even though the Franciscans are not mentioned in the sources in connection with these performances.

14. *Der schauspielerische Stil*, p. 117.

15. The following section on Villingen war originally published under the "Der Villinger Bühnenplan" in *The Journal of English and Germanic Philology* 54 (1955): 318–31. It is reprinted here in translation with permission of the University of Illinois Press.

16. *Schauspiele des Mittelalters* (Karlsruhe, 1846), 2:156.

17. G. Dinges, *Untersuchungen zum Donaueschinger Passionsspiel* (Breslau, 1910).

18. Christian Roder, "Ehemalige Passionsspiele zu Villingen," *Freiburger Diözesan-Archiv*, n. s., 17 (1916): 163–92.

19. Quoted from the diary of Abbott George Gaisser of St. Georgen by J. Bolte, "Handschriftliche Dramen in Donaueschingen," *Zeitschrift für deutsches Altertum* 32 (1888): 1.

In the introduction to his edition of the Donaueschingen Passion Play, Mone published a "copy" of the stage plan,[20] which radically touches up the rough outlines of the drawing. Froning was the first to reproduce the original drawing in its primary form.[21] Nonetheless, later theater historians preferred to busy themselves with Mone's incorrect copy.[22] The single scholar to turn his attention to the original drawing was M. Blakemore Evans;[23] to a certain extent, he was rewarded for his efforts. Of course, Albert Rapp also concerned himself with the original, but only to make an attempt straightway to place his copy of the original drawing over the ground plan of a church.[24]

In his day, Mone was struck by the fact that the written characters on the stage plan came from the sixteenth century, while the manuscript of the Donaueschingen Passion Play had been prepared in the fifteenth century. From these circumstances Mone drew the conclusion that the stage plan represented the scenic arrangement for a performance of the Donaueschingen Passion Play in the sixteenth century. Nonetheless, he also noticed that the stage sketch did not fit the text of the plan—in fact, that it was in direct contradiction of the list of "hüsser vnd höff" needed for the performance of the play as given on leaf 1ʳ of Manuscript 137. A number of the stations indicated in the list were simply not to be found on the stage sketch. After he had ascertained that the stage sketch "contains by no means as many objects as are indicated at the opening of the play," Mone gave the following explanation: "In later performances, then, the play was shortened, just as is still done in the theater today."[25]

Froning was the first scholar to doubt the connection of the stage plan with the Donaueschingen Passion Play: "The sketch does not belong to the play in the form in which the latter has come down to us; rather, it comes from a later time and has been added to the manuscript on a loose leaf."[26] Froning did not try at all, then, to make the text of the Donaueschingen Passion Play fit the Procrustes bed of the stage plan.

In 1910, Dinges became convinced that the stage plan did not belong to the Donaueschingen Passion Play: "It matches handsomely with the text of the VP [Villingen Passion Play]."[27] Of all the scholars who have worked with the stage plan,

20. *Schauspiele des Mittelalters,* 2:156.
21. Froning, *Das Drama des Mittelalters,* following p. 276.
22. For instance, Chambers, *The Mediaeval Stage,* 2:84, and E. Hartl, ed., *Das Drama des Mittelalters* (Leipzig, 1942), 4:12.
23. "The Staging of the Donaueschingen Passion Play," *Modern Language Review* 15 (1920): 65–76, 279–97.
24. *Studien über den Zusammenhang des geistlichen Dramas mit der bildenden Kunst* (Kallmünz, 1936).
25. *Schauspiele des Mittelalters,* 2:155.
26. Froning, *Das Drama des Mittelalters,* p. 277.
27. *Untersuchungen zum Donaueschinger Passionsspiel,* p. 135.

Dinges was the only one to compare Manuscripts 137 and 138; in addition, he published stage directions, textual samples, and a detailed synopsis of the unpublished Villingen Passion Play. But Dinges, too, failed to delve into the connection of the stage plan with the Villingen Passion Play. He merely observed that the stage plan did not provide for a Temple, although the Temple was required in the opening scenes of the Villingen Passion in its manuscript form. Dinges provided the following explanation for its absence: "On the plan, only the location of the temple is missing; however, we should not be surprised that it has been forgotten in this hasty sketch, since it appears only in scenes 2 and 3 of the First Act; if we place it between Herod's house and the room for the Last Supper, a nice symmetry results."[28] I shall propose another solution to the riddle of the missing Temple below.

Dinges's statement—that the stage plan does not fit the Donaueschingen Passion Play, but is suited to the Villingen Passion—made no impression at first. In his Frankfurt lectures of 1917, Julius Petersen still spoke of the "Donaueschingen plan," and adduced a woodcut by Vogtherr in his publication, saying that it would give us "an idea of how the areas for Golgotha and Jerusalem were separated by a wall and a gate."[29] The notion of "wall and gate" has subsequently had a fateful effect upon scholarship. Otherwise, Petersen avoided using the expression "Donaueschingen stage plan" in his essay on the stage of the older Frankfurt Passion Play, and, making reference to Dinges, spoke of the Villingen plan. Meanwhile, M. Blakemore Evans devoted a paper to the production of the Donaueschingen Passion Play. Although he was familiar with the work of Dinges, Evans proceeded all the same from the assumption that the manuscript stage plan was intended for the Donaueschingen Passion Play. While so doing, he came to the conclusion that "the sketch represents the action of the second day only."[30] In the execution of his hypothesis, Evans was by no means in an enviable position. It was a question of making the text of the Donaueschingen Passion Play and the list of houses and courts given on leaf 1ʳ of the manuscript harmonize with the sketch. The text and the list show no essential discrepancies, something which in and of itself should make us inclined to regard the list of the stage locations as official and allow us, with its aid, to carry out the reconstruction of the Donaueschingen Passion Play in about the same manner, say, as Petersen did in the case of the older Frankfurt Passion Play. Unfortunately (one is almost tempted to say), the loose leaf was enclosed with the manuscript of the Donaueschingen play, onto which a much later hand had scribbled a stage plan, so that now the list of the

28. Ibid.
29. *Das deutsche Nationaltheater* (Leipzig and Berlin, 1919), pp. 8–9.
30. "The Staging of the Donaueschingen Passion Play," p. 283.

stage localities and the text suporting the list had to be made to fit the stage plan—
by hook or by crook.

Evans believed that he had done away with a part of the difficulties when he came
to the firm conclusion that the stage plan reproduced the arrangement of the second
day alone. This was not accomplished without some acts of violence. In the mansion
list of the manuscript there appeared "Der berg, da der tüffel got versucht" and "Der
ölberg" as two different stage localities; but Evans could not resist the temptation of
combining the two raised places in one.[31] While "die appenteck" was clearly defined
in the list as a stage locality and was used as such on both days of the Donaueschingen
Passion Play, Evans reduced the importance of the *unguentarius* station: the apothecary "at most would require merely a place on the stage."[32] But even "merely a place"
would have to be indicated on a stage plan, if a stage plan were to have any meaning
at all, and Cysat did not fail to include the apothecary in his stage plan. Evans had still
other difficulties to surmount. The sketch did not provide a place for Christ and the
disciples. The Temple was also missing, as well as a house in which the Christians
who were not apostles could meet. These are all stage locations which the second day
of the Donaueschingen play required and for which provision had been made in the
list, where we find not only the Temple mentioned, but also "Der zwölffbotten huss"
and "Der christenen huss." Evans has no explanation for the absence of these houses
from the stage plan, and he finally takes refuge in Cysat's stage plan, where it may
be assumed "with some probability" that the places for the Savior and the disciples,
for the Temple, and for Lazarus and his circle were arranged for the Donaueschingen
play in about the same way as they appear on the Lucerne plans. Evans even went so
far as to write, "Indeed these Lucerne plans, modified to meet the somewhat different
requirements of the text and sketch, furnish a reconstruction of the Donaueschingen
stage more accurate than any we might attempt."[33] It hardly provides cause for aston-
ishment, then, when Evans concludes by declaring that the reconstruction of the
Donaueschingen Passion stage would be "a fairly easy matter" on the basis of the
existing material.

I believe that Evans was too optimistic. Having attempted a reconstruction of this
sort, he arrived at erroneous conclusions because he proceeded from the fallacious
premise that the stage plan fits the second day of the Donaueschingen Passion. All the
same, Evans's reconstruction was not wholly in vain. His study afforded us one positive

31. Ibid., p. 282, n. 4: I have been sorely tempted to identify . . . the 'berg' of Temptation with
the 'Ölberg' of the second day."
32. Ibid., n. 2.
33. Ibid., p. 283.

development: he ignored the copy made by Mone and turned to the original sketch of the stage plan. In the process, something caught his attention which was bound to escape everyone who worked only with the copy—that the third section of the drawing (Golgotha, the graves, and Heaven) appeared to be divided from the second section by two parallel diagonal lines. In these two diagonals from the hand of a clumsy draftsman Evans saw an attempt to indicate the elevated site of the third section. Considering the large number of graves, this elevated site would be of the greatest value; the opportunity to use trapdoors would be of particular advantage for the person acting the Savior's role, since he had to make a subterranean change of costume between the burial and harrowing of Hell. Of course, it is impossible to understand why Evans was inclined to assume that such an elevated site also existed for the first section, although he could find no support for his theory in the original sketch.

The extant stage plan was not intended for a production of the Donaueschingen Passion Play: it belongs to the later Villingen play. The proof for this assertion must begin with a stage location which, to my knowledge, none of the interpreters has recognized as such, and yet this location is plainly entered on the stage sketch and given a caption there. I am thinking of the middle arch, denoted as "das tor." Most interpreters after Mone busied themselves too much with numbering "die tore"; following Mone's lead, they registered the location—denoted as "das tor" on the stage plan—as "second gate," overlooking the fact that there are no first and third gates on the sketch but rather only, centrally located, "das tor." Evans slides past "das tor" with the phrase "which may be disregarded." I believe that scholarship has hitherto been wrong in paying no attention to this particular "tor," for it holds the key to the explanation of the stage plan and to its identification with the Villingen Passion Play.

Taken large, the Villingen Passion Play corresponds to the second day of the Donaueschingen play. But—not having had the chance to examine the manuscript of the Villingen play—if we follow the table of contents of the Villingen Passion as provided by Dinges, we shall discover a couple of differences all the same, of which only one needs to be stressed at the moment: the Villingen manuscript contains a scene that is not in the Donaueschingen Passion. It is the episode in which the maid tending the door refuses to admit Peter into the court of the high priest: "But Peter was standing at the door without. So the other disciple, who was known unto the high priest, went out and spake unto her that kept the door, and brought in Peter. The maid therefore that kept the door saith unto Peter: Art thou also one of this man's disciples? He saith, I am not" (John 18:16–17). Now I assume that the stage location denoted as "das tor" served as the place of this scene, which led to the first denial. Since the scene

Stage plan for a Passion play production at Villingen (between 1585 and 1600). Original in the Fürstlich Fürstenbergische Bibliothek, Donaueschingen.

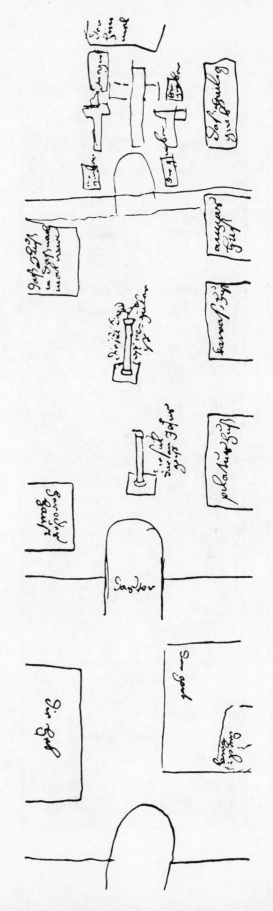

Hubert Cailleau's miniature for the eighteenth day of the Valenciennes Passion (1547), from the MS Rothschild 1.7.3 in the Bibliothèque Nationale, Paris. It clearly shows the kind of gate which I
postulate for the "tor" on the Villingen plan.

does not appear in the Donaueschingen Passion, the list of stage locations of Manuscript 137 does not call for a "tor."

Naturally, we may only guess at the appearance of the gate. A lattice between two doorposts might have sufficed to suggest what it was. After all, the view of the spectators could not be cut off by solid structures, of the sort Petersen appears to have deduced from the Vogtherr woodcut.[34] And yet the Vogtherr woodcut can be of aid to us here, if we move our eyes from the right side's walls and stone arches toward the left, where a "tor" constructed of three beams is visible, with a kind of low fence runing out from it toward the right.[35] On Cysat's stage plans we find archlike indications of gates in the three corners, accompanied by Cysat's directive: "Ein beschlossen durchsichtig Thor oder gatter." A low fence, leading diagonally across the stage to the left and the right of the posts, may have divided the first section from the second in Villingen. At the arrest of Jesus in the first part, all the disciples fled, and John, whose mantel the Jews snatched in the Villingen Passion, ran into the second section. Judas accompanied the bailiffs who led the Savior into the second section, and to the house of Annas. Peter stayed behind in the first section. The maid posted herself at the "tor" and closed the lattice. While Christ stood before Annas, Peter attempted to enter the second section, at which point the above-described scene with the maid and John took place. The scene resembled the same episode in Jean Michel's *Passion,* where a "Chamberiere" refused to grant Peter admittance. Michel's stage direction runs: "Ycy entre Saint Jehan, et Saint Pierre demaure a l'uys." After John's intervention, Peter is allowed to pass through the gate (*huis*).[36]

I mentioned the two doorposts between which the lattice may have been hung. I deduce the existence of such posts from the scene of Judas's self-destruction, although I am fully aware of the purely hypothetical character of my assumption. But no one as yet has pondered the fact that the "ski lift" on which Judas goes to Hell must have been hooked up at two points. The one of these points, naturally, was Hell, the goal of the suicide's journey. But where was the other point, to which the rope for the suspension equipment was also attached? It is perhaps not too daring to assert that in the Villingen Passion Play the exact stage directions for the death of Judas are missing, while the Donaueschingen play notes all the technical details at precisely this junc-

34. Hans Heinrich Borcherdt, *Das europäische Theater im Mittelalter und in der Renaissance* (Leipzig, 1935), p. 19, likewise speaks of "a middle section enclosed by walls and gates." Dörrer, in *Verfasserlexikon* vol. 3, col. 720, suggests a symbolic interpretation: "in the middle the terrestrial world, to one side Hell, to the other Heaven."

35. Cailleau's miniature for the eighteenth day of the Valenciennes Passion clearly shows such a gate.

36. See the scene in Gustave Cohen, *Le livre de conduite,* pp. 294–95.

ture.[37] (The wording of the suicide monologue in the Villingen play, however, coincides perfectly with that of the Donaueschingen Passion.) Naturally we do not know if a ladder was used in Villingen too, of the sort provided for in the Donaueschingen play, but at any event the lattice gave the suicide the means of lifting himself from the ground, while Beelzebub (in Villingen, instead of the Belzebock of Manuscript 137), who had climbed up onto the post in advance, waited for Judas with the noose. Thereupon the two of them glided down to Hell together.

Now let us turn to the two "other gates," about which there is some discussion in all the explanations. The arch entered on the left side of the sketch appears to indicate the entrance to the space set aside for the spectators, and to the stage: this was the limit of the space for the theater on the left, just as Heaven represented the limit on the right. This was the entrance for the spectators, and, once they were in their places, for the procession of the amateur actors. I suspect that the gate indicated here is the one providing admittance to the cloister garden of the Franciscans. According to Roder,[38] the Villingen performances took place in the Franciscans' garden on the south side of the monastery.

In my opinion, the "third gate" was simply the point indicated with an archlike drawing by the draftsman, at which (according to Evans) the elevated third division of the stage was entered upon. We may reckon here with the installation of steps (as in Lucerne, in front of the fountain stage) or of a ramp.

My interpretation may be called a prosaic one, but I think it is necessary that a sobering note be introduced, since, for earlier interpreters, the "three gates" achieved a significance that was downright mystical. Chambers believed it was permissible to regard the three sections as corresponding to the three parts of a church.[39] Rapp even went to the trouble of transposing the stage plan onto the "normal interior of a church," providing the following explanation: "Let us take, then, a simple church interior as the original basis of this arrangement, as has been done in the accompanying redrawing: the gates reveal themselves as the arches of the middle aisle which, seen from the laiety's part of the church, gave access to the three sections of the space

37. *Untersuchungen zum Donaueschinger Passionsspiel,* p. 132. See the stage directions in Hartl, *Das Drama des Mittelalters,* 4:188, 190: "Hie sol Judas böum oder ein leiter zů gerüst sin, vnd ein seil dar von bitz in die hell gespannen, mit schiben wol versorgt . . . vnd gat der tüffel vor im die leiter vff vnd zögt im allweg den strick, vnd gat im Judas nach vff. . . . Vff dissen spruch leit Belzebock dem Judas den strick an vnd versorgt in wol am haggen vnd setzt sich den hinder in vff ein bengel . . . den farent sy beyd zů der hell."
38. "Ehemalige Passionsspiele zu Villingen," p. 177.
39. *The Mediaeval Stage,* 2:84. Also A. Nicoll, *Masks, Mimes and Miracles* (London, 1931), p. 198.

reserved for the priests during the high holidays.... The church, conceived of as a holy highway, thus determined once and for all the progress and the pauses of the action."[40] Hans Rueff was of the opinion that "a sure awareness of dramatic organization" reveals itself in the stage plan: "The gates, taken as boundaries between the acts, separate three phases of intensity. The playwright must be given credit for having discovered that, with his stage, which is oriented quite simply toward the chronology of events, he might faithfully reproduce the structure of the story of the passion, which rises in an unbroken line toward its supreme events. As a matter of fact, he has succeeded in making the sketch of the stage correspond to the pattern of inner connections in the story of the redemption."[41]

Finally, Eduard Hartl made an attempt to bring the sketch of the stage plan into agreement with the Donaueschingen Passion Play. Without referring to Evans, Hartl also offered the explanation that, as far as the sketch was concerned, it was "only a case of presenting the stage localities required on the second day."[42] It evidently did not bother him in the least that, according to the stage direction before verse 2395, Judas enters into the Temple, which, however, does not appear on the stage sketch at all. Nor was Hartl especially disturbed by the absence of a position for the vendor of ointments on the sketch, although "die appenteck" is expressly enumerated as a "huss" in the introductory list. "No fixed stage location is necessary for the 'Appenteck,' which was put in some free space or other, in other words, in a 'hoff': a table, a chair, and some ointment boxes may well have sufficed for the purpose."[43] On the second day, however, the Donaueschingen play needed not only the Temple and the apothecary's shop, but also a place of assembly for the Christian party, a place for the three Marys, for Joseph of Arimathea, for Nicodemus, and for Peter, whom the Marys tell about the Resurrection—and we do not know what was called for in the missing six pages of the Donaueschingen manuscript (perhaps the appearance of Christ before the disciples, as Dinges[44] assumed, following the Lucerne version of 1545). In all three cases (Temple, apothecary's shop, house of the Christians or disciples), Hartl simply passes over the difficulties which must arise when one examines the stage plan in conjunction with the Donaueschingen Passion, without getting rid of them. In what follows, it will be shown that the difficulties disappear when we connect the stage plan not with the Donaueschingen play but with that of Villingen.

40. Rapp, *Studien über den Zusammenhang*, pp. 60, 63 (the drawing on p. 62).
41. *Das rheinische Osterspiel*, p. 45.
42. Hartl, *Das Drama des Mittelalters*, 4:13. Hartl persisted in staring at Mone's schematic redrawing.
43. Ibid.
44. *Untersuchungen zum Donaueschinger Passionsspiel*, pp. 144–53.

In the first place, the Temple. As already indicated, Dinges[45] explains its absence by referring to the "haste" with which the draftsman prepared his sketch, a haste which seems excusable to Dinges because the Temple in Villingen was used only in the second and third scene of the play. I find this theory of haste and the reasoning behind it untenable, for the draftsman did not forget to enter the pillar with the cock on his sketch, even though the cock swung into action in but a single episode. Perhaps the absence of the Temple on the sketch could be explained in another way, after all. From Dinges's précis of the Villingen Passion it becomes evident that Christ entered into Jerusalem and lamented the city's fate in the first scene. In the second scene we have the cleansing of the Temple, in the third the scene between Christ and the adulteress, in the fourth the Jews appear before Caiaphas, and in the fifth the decision to slay Christ is made. I am inclined to assume that the stage plan referred to a performance of the Villingen Passion in which the first three scenes were cut. In the performance for which the stage plan was intended, the play may have begun with the scene where the Jews, gathered before the house of Caiaphas (in the Caiaphas mansion), decided to kill Christ. One can hardly imagine a better beginning for a play concentrated on the suffering, death, and Resurrection of Christ—in striking contrast to the Donaueschingen play, where the scenes with Mary Magdalene, the miracle cures, and the various disputes of Christ with the Jews are included. The entrance into Jerusalem, the cleansing of the Temple, and the scene with the adulteress belong to the preamble of the Passion, it is not out of the question that the single remnants of the preamble (the cleansing of the Temple and the adulteress) were removed in the Villingen performance for which the stage plan was intended. This would offer an adequate explanation, at any event, for the absence of the Temple from the plan. The omission of the opening scenes made the Temple superfluous, and as a result the house of Annas appears to have formed the assembly place of the Jews. While the Jewish school was lodged in the mansion of Caiaphas, and Judas cast down the money before the Jews in the house of Caiaphas or Annas, Christ made his first appearance in the eighth scene (in Dinges's numbering), in which he prophesied his suffering and commanded the disciples to prepare the Last Supper.

Now let us turn to the missing apothecary's shop. Evans and Hartl, staring fixedly at the Donaueschingen Passion, thought of a solution with an improved location. But Dinges reports[46] that the Villingen Passion, in contrast to Donaueschingen's, has no mercator scene at all. Thus the Villingen stage plan has not provided a location for

45. Ibid., p. 135.
46. Ibid., p. 143.

the apothecary scene (not even an improvised one), since Villingen got along without an apothecary. Once again, the stage plan does not suit the Donaueschingen play (not even its second day); it does suit the later Villingen play.

Even though I have not examined the manuscript of the Villingen Passion, I believe that I have proved, on the basis of the information imparted by Dinges, that in the so-called Donaueschingen stage plan we in fact are confronted with the sketch for a performance of the Villingen Passion.

Wolfgang F. Michael[47] has confused the situation anew by looking for gates and walls in Villingen. It is not surprising that he found a city wall, four main gates, a moat, and outworks. Thereupon he came to regard the Villingen plan as a sketch for the performance of a processional play which took place on the main street, running east and west, and which included the city moat and the eastern outworks. I can only call Michael's attempted correction of my Villingen interpretation absurd. When he asserts that "the double notation, 'der graben,' immediately to the right and the left behind the third gate, points quite unambiguously to the city moat," he overlooks the fact that not two but rather four little rectangles have been entered between the three crosses, something which would be an extremely unlikely draftsman's method for capturing the existence of a city moat. Nor would I move the "heilig grab" so lightly into the "city moat." What is indicated here by clumsy illustrative means is simply a raised stage, into which trapdoors were placed, making the entombment of Christ technically possible, as well as the resurrection of the dead at his death. Together with Mone, I read "die greber"; and so we are rid of Michael's ill-fated moat.

BOZEN (1514)

Vigil Raber's stage plan for the Palm Sunday Play of the Bozen Passion Cycle of 1514 was accessible for almost a century only in Adolf Pichler's strongly normalized copy.[48] Before the original disappeared, M. Blakemore Evans had traced the sketch and passed it on to his dissertation candidate, Reinhold Nordsieck, for an evaluation. Finally Nordsieck published a reproduction, faithful to the original, in an essay.[49]

The performance of the *Vorspiel,* as well as of the remaining six parts of the cycle, took place in the town church. Nordsieck traced Raber's plan over the ground plan of the church, and in the process arrived at improbably modest proportions both for

47. *Frühformen der deutschen Bühne,* pp. 50–51.
48. *Über das Drama des Mittelalters in Tirol* (Innsbruck, 1850).
49. "Der Bühnenplan des Vigil Raber: ein Beitrag zur Bühnengeschichte des Mittelalters," *Monatshefte für deutschen Unterricht* (M. Blakemore Evans Festschrift) 37 (1945): 114–29.

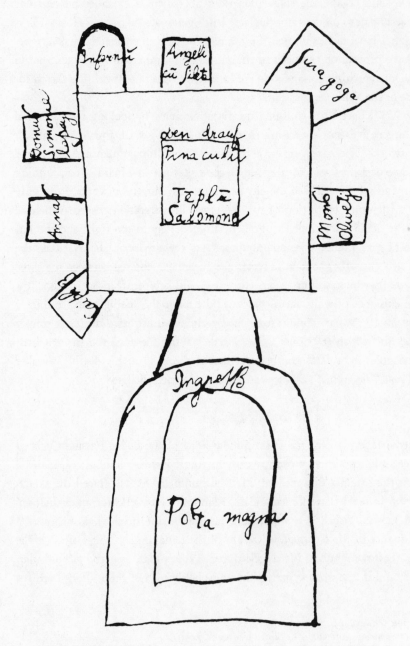

Vigil Raber's stage plan for the church performance of Part I of the Passion play in Bozen, Palm Sunday, 1514.

the stage area and for the single mansions. To be more precise: he squeezed Raber's plan into the part of the church "directly in front of the choir, between the rows of columns which form the middle aisle."[50] The dimensions of the central stage area dwindled thereby to a mere 9.6 by 8.54 meters.[51] Objecting to his, Michael undertook to make the necessary improvements on Nordsieck's reconstruction in an essay of his own.[52] In Michael's opinion, Nordsieck's stage was "much too small," because the *Vorspiel* required no less than seventy-five participants, far too large a number to be accommodated on Nordsieck's podium. The house of Simon Leprosus alone, for which Nordsieck calculated measurements of 2.55 by 1.91 meters, had to hold seventeen persons, not to mention the table and the benches. On this account, Michael enlarged the stage by extending it to include the whole breadth of the church, thus not only the middle aisle but also the two side aisles. In this way, about half of the church became stage space. Aided by the rubrics, Michael then laid out a scheme for the performance of the *Vorspiel.* His "promptbook" does not, of course, possess absolute authority, since other solutions are also conceivable. For the performances on the other days we have no aid in the form of drawings, and we cannot get very far on the stage directions alone.

"The Castle of Perseverance"

The Macro Manuscript (ca. 1425) has transmitted the text of an English morality play, *The Castle of Perseverance,* to posterity. The play is accompanied by a stage plan which provides suggestions concerning the form of performance. In an effort to interpret the diagram, Richard Southern[53] has woven a net of thought whose meshes are large indeed.

Let us turn to the sketch. The Castle of Perseverance stands in the middle of two concentric circles, an edifice beneath which there is a bed for the birth of the "human soul." The area within the circles itself is designated as "Place." The two circles indicate a ditch, filled with water, which can also be replaced by a palisade. The ditch, or the fence, seems to have the purpose of controlling the admission of the spectators. On the periphery of the outer circle, positions for five mansions are sketched in; the house for Caro is in the south, Mundus is located in the west, Belial dwells in the north, and Coveytyse in the northwest; the Heavenly Paradise stands in the east. In

50. Ibid., p. 124.
51. Dörrer, in *Verfasserlexikon,* vol. 3, col. 814, assumes a platform size of 10 m².
52. "The Staging of the Bozen Passion Play," *The Germanic Review* 25 (1950): 178–95.
53. *The Medieval Theatre in the Round* (London, 1957).

addition, the stage plan gives instructions concerning the colors of the costumes for the four "daughters of God." The actor of the Devil's role is required to have explosive torches in his hands, ears, and backside. A limited number of "stytelerys" officiated in the "Place," a mysterious group of functionaries, whom Southern identifies as ushers. Southern gave these "ushers" the task of controlling the spectators (who, according to his opinion, were in the "Place") so that the actors would not be disturbed in their movements. Glynne Wickham[54] entertains justified doubts about Southern's theory. In the circumstance that the stage plan does not provide for spectators to be in the "Place," Wickham sees an indication that they were just outside the stage area, in other words, the platea. In any case, we are confronted here with a theater-in-the-round, a form whose existence is also established in the case of the Cornwall miracle plays.

The stage plan provides no information concerning the appearance of the marginal mansions. They seem to have been elevated, since the verbs *ascendere* and *descendere* appear frequently in the rubrics. At this point, Southern looked for analogies in Fouquet's miniature, *The Martyrdom of Saint Apollonia,* where the mansions are elevated and rendered accessible by a ramp or ladder.

But, once again, the stage plan and the rubrics only make the limits of our knowledge apparent. Southern exceeds these limits by asking, and then answering, the question, what happened with the earth which had to be dug out in order to make the trench? Southern is of the opinion that it was used for building up a circular earthen rampart, the inner slope of which was transformed into an amphitheater for the spectators. Thus we have arrived in Cornwall, the homeland of "earthen amphitheaters." Of course, *The Castle of Perseverance* has nothing to do with Cornwall. Let us return to the stage plan once more. The text accompanying the drawing speaks only of a ditch or, a second possibility, of a solid enclosure. ("strongly barryd al abowt"). There is no talk of an earthen rampart; that is a fiction on Southern's part. It is reasonable to assume that the morality was acted by a troupe of strolling players. Two mounted standard-bearers appeared in the town a few days before the planned production and announced the performance, which would take place on the "green." Southern's assumption that in every town the troupe dug a ditch, ten feet broad and five feet deep, simply takes the wrong track. The last editor of the Macro Plays, Mark Eccles,[55] expressed understandable skepticism: "I doubt that so large a ditch was needed and that loose earth would make very good seats."

54. *The Medieval Theatre* (New York, 1974), p. 117.
55. *The Macro Plays,* Early English Text Society, 240 (Oxford, 1969), p. xxiii.

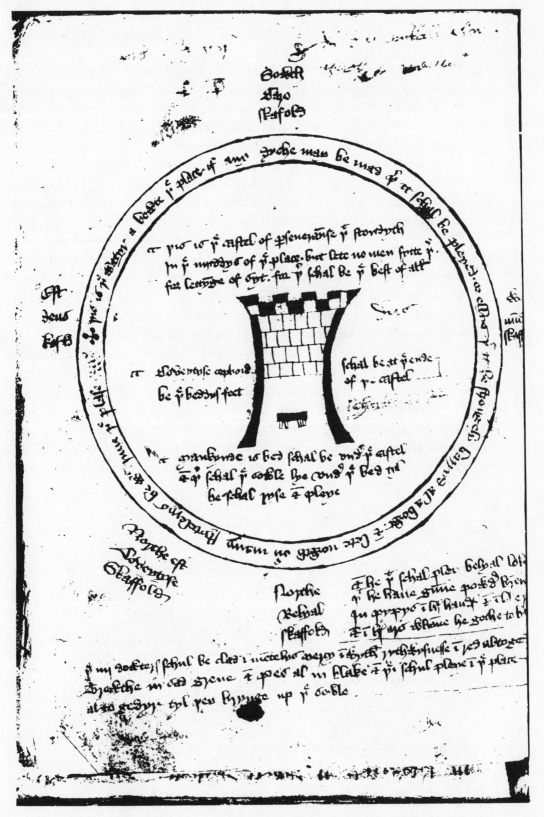

Ground plan for an unidentified performance of the morality *The Castle of Perseverance* (ca. 1425).
By permission of the Folger Shakespeare Library, Washington, D.C.

Natalie Crohn Schmitt[56] has submitted an interpretation of the enigmatic stage plan which differs radically from Southern's theory. Miss Schmitt detects not just a ditch but a castle's moat surrounding the Castle of Perseverance. In the drawing, she sees the "stage picture" of a castle enclosed within a moat in the form of a ring. She places the mansions outside the circle, an arrangement for which the sketch seems to provide. For Schmitt, the moat is only symbolic, not being either very deep or very broad, and whatever earth was dug out of it was simply carted away. To support her theory Schmitt cites from homiletic literature medieval notions of allegorical castles, such as the castle of the Virgin Mary, surrounded by the "Water of Virtues" or the "Water of her Tears." For Schmitt, water is also the symbol of purification in the baptism. It appears to me that this allegorical interpretation is rather farfetched. It offers no explanation for the presence of the "stytelerys" in the "place." It can scarcely be assumed that spectators crossed this allegorical moat if it was intended as a part of the castle itself. And what happens to all that precious water if, as an alternative, the stage plan indicates that a strong fence will also be quite satisfactory?

In any case, Southern's reconstruction has more often been accepted than rejected; as a matter of fact, a whole theater-in-the-round epidemic began. Everything was crammed, then, into "the round," every platea was forced into a circular mold.[57]

Authentic circular stage plans are available for the Cornish *Ordinalia.* These diagrams, in conjunction with the rubrics and William Borlase's sketch of Piran Round, allow us to retrace the arena staging of the Cornish Cycle with considerable certainty. Neville Denny has combined caution with fervor in his exemplary resurrection of the *Passio Domini.*[58]

THE DIGBY "MARY MAGDALENE"

Although no official stage plan is available for the play, it may be mentioned in this connection all the same, since the circular form is also under debate here. The circle theory had already been developed for *Mary Magdalene,* even before the ap-

56. "Was There a Medieval Theatre in the Round?," *Theatre Notebook* 23 (1968/69): 130–42. Catherine Belsey, "The Stage Plan of *The Castle of Perseverance*," *Theatre Notebook* 28 (1974): 124–32, challenged Miss Schmitt's central thesis and voiced justified doubts concerning her symbolic moat interpretation. However, Miss Belsey replaces one allegorical interpretation with still another.

57. The disease is contagious; only recently it struck France when Henri Rey-Flaud, *Le cercle magique, essay sur le théâtre en rond à la fin du Moyen Age* (Paris, 1973), pp. 167–73, 192–222, attempted, by gross misinterpretation of the available sources, to place the Romans performance of 1509 and the Valenciennes Passion of 1547 into a "dispositif en rond."

58. "Arena Staging and Dramatic Quality in the Cornish Passion Play," in *Medieval Drama,* ed. Neville Denny, Stratford-upon-Avon Studies 16 (London 1973): 124–53.

pearance of Southern's book. When F. J. Furnivall published the play in 1882, he had no very clear idea of the conditions of performance. His view had been influenced by Thomas Sharp,[59] to the effect that pageant wagons were employed. Later on, E. K. Chambers entertained a vision of an "elaborate stationary mise en scene with various loca."[60] Then, J. Q. Adams[61] took up the idea of a circular form and prepared a scheme for the first 925 verses by which eight mansions on the periphery of a circle would have surrounded a central plateau. From his diagram it is not evident where he thought the public would be—outside the circle or within it?

Finally, Victor Albright[62] transposed the stage plan of *The Castle* onto the Magdalene play. The castle stood in the center of the *Castle* plan. That is where Albright placed the mansion for Cyrus. He put eleven loca around the periphery of the circle and surrounded the circle with a moat, filled with water, on which the ship made its passage to Marseilles. A trench arrangement of this sort would have caused considerable expenditures of work and money, quite without any justification, as long as a ship on wheels could move over dry, flat ground.

Hardin Craig returned to Adams's idea: "This stage was apparently round, like that of *The Castle of Perseverance,* with spectators viewing it from all sides."[63] Martial Rose[64] also belonged to Adams's school of thought.

One of my students, Gary Jay Williams, presented in a seminar paper convincing arguments against the circle theory, by demonstrating that this Digby play could be staged with mansions arranged in a half-circle. Following the lead of Harry M. Ritchie,[65] he thought Lincoln the likely place of performance. The language of the play points to an origin in the East Midlands, with Lincoln as the religious focal point. The city had a long tradition of spiritual plays, the organization of which lay in the hands of Saint Anne's Guild.[66] The majority of the performances seem to have taken place beside or within the cathedral. Ritchie drew attention to the fact that there was a chapel of Mary Magdalene in the cathedral close, in which the relics of the saint were venerated. The entrance to the cathedral square was made through two gates, an outer and an inner one. The area between them was called "the Chequer." Ritchie expressed the opinion that "the courtyard of the Chequer gates or the court-

59. Thomas Sharp, ed., *Ancient Mysteries from the Digby Manuscipts* (Edinburgh, 1835).
60. *The Mediaeval Stage,* 2:430.
61. John Q. Adams, ed., *Chief Pre-Shakespearean Dramas* (Boston, 1924), p. 225.
62. *The Shakespearean Stage* (New York, 1909), pp. 15–17.
63. *English Religious Drama,* p. 316.
64. *The Wakefield Mystery Plays,* p. 35.
65. "A Suggested Location for the Digby *Mary Magdalene,*" *Theatre Survey* 4 (1963): 51–58.
66. Craig, *English Religious Drama,* p. 275.

yard of the minster proper" could be considered for the performance. Williams followed Ritchie to the cathedral, but he saw no possibility for a performance inside the
Chequer's small space. He moved the play into the great cathedral close (or minster
yard), regarding the eastern facade of the inner gate as the background against
which the mansions were arranged in a half-circle.[67] The smaller inner courtyard
gave an opportunity for preparing such scenes as the appearance of Christ or the
rolling-in of the ship. Technical apparatus, such as was necessary for Mary Magdalene's ascent into the clouds of Heaven, would have been supported by the stonework
of the gate. The spectators turned their backs to the western portal of the cathedral.

67. Cameron and Kahrl, "Staging the N.-Town Cycle," pp. 136–37, offer fairly exact measurements
for the Minster Close: "The west front of the Cathedral is one hundred and forty-four feet wide,
while the entire area is about two hundred and five feet wide; it is about one hundred and ten feet
deep, from Exchequer Gate to the Cathedral front. Of the approximately twenty-two thousand five
hundred square feet in this area, about six thousand are taken up by the line of houses, leaving about
sixteen thousand five hundred square feet of usable space."

4   Processional or Stationary?

AN OPEN QUESTION. An attempt to answer it will only lead us into the thickest underbrush of revocable surmises. When English philology began to concern itself with the English mystery plays (in other words, since Thomas Sharp), there was but one thesis: the cycles of Chester, York, Coventry, and Wakefield were performed in processional fashion, that is, within the cities just named, certain stations were chosen at which the individual plays of the cycle were given, or repeated, on "pageant wagons" entrusted to the care of the guilds. The performances took place at Whitsuntide or the Feast of Corpus Christi. The number of stopping places depended on the topographical circumstances.

CHESTER

The main source supporting the orthodox procession theory for Chester is a description by David Rogers in his *Breviarye,* a local history of Chester. F. M. Salter[1] has asserted that David Rogers cannot be considered an eyewitness, since he wrote his local history in 1609, thirty-four years after the last performance in Chester for which we have any evidence (1575). We do not know how old Rogers was when he composed his history. But one must take the possibility into account, all the same, that he employed impressions from his youth, or at the least gathered information from older citizens, in particular from his father, Robert Rogers. It could be learned from his report concerning the performance of the Chester Cycle that its twenty-four plays (twenty-five in 1574) were performed at five points in the city. The cycle was divided into three days: nine plays on Whitmonday, eight (nine in 1574) on Tuesday, seven on Wednesday.

Salter arrived at the hypothesis that the original Chester Cycle was given in a "stationary" form and assumed its processional mode only later. However skeptical he was toward Rogers' testimony, Salter nevertheless clung to the processional theory. Rogers named five points within the city as stations for the performances: at the Abbey Gate, at the High Cross, in Watergate Street, Bridgegate Street, and Eastgate Street.[2] Without giving any reasons for his decision, Salter decided that there were

---

1. *Medieval Drama in Chester* (Toronto, 1955), p. 55.
2. This is the *Breviarye* reading in the version of Harley MS 1944. Harley MS 1948 actually mentions only stations at the Abbey Gate and High Cross; other stops are merely hinted at: "and so to euery streete."

four points instead: at the Abbey, at the High Cross, in front of Chester Castle, and finally on the Roodee (Rood Eye), a meadow outside the city walls which served as a drill ground but was also the site of horse races and occasional performances by mimics. Rogers stated that the pageant wagons followed one another smoothly, without any interruption: "And thus they came from one streete to an other keapeinge a direct order in euery streete, for before the first cariage was gone the seconde came, and so the thirde, and so orderly till the laste was donne all in order without any stayeinge in any place" (Harley MS 1944).

Meanwhile, the procession theory was submitted to a process of revision. Leonard Powlick[3] expressed his doubts about the possibility of the Chester Cycle being done in a processional fashion. He voiced the opinion that the performances did not take place in the streets of the city, but rather outside the walls, on the Roodee meadow. On the city map of Chester, drawn in 1610 by John Speed, Powlick detected a natural rise ("a sheer bluff of some fifty feet") on the Rood Eye. The elevator which aided Christ on his ascent into Heaven could be installed against this incline. Jesus sang as he began his climb ("Tunc Iesus Ascendit et in ascendendo cantabit"). He did not go straight up to Heaven but stopped halfway ("in medio quasi supra nubes") in order to receive the adoration of the angels. Then he completed his journey ("Tunc Ascendet"), while two angels descended and asked the apostles, "Quid aspicitis in Coelum?"[4]

Powlick could not reconcile himself to Rogers's processional arrangement because a smooth continuity of the plays could only be guaranteed if all the plays were more or less the same size. In Chester this was certainly not the case. The first play, *Lucifer's Fall*, has a length of 280 verses. However, the second, *The Creation*, has 704 verses. Then comes *The Flood* with 372 verses. How could Rogers assert that there was no "stayeing," "no place to tarye"? The spectators in front of the abbey could see Plays I, II, and III in unbroken succession. But the good people (among them the mayor himself) who meant to watch the performance at the High Cross had to wait a considerable time after the conclusion of *Lucifer's Fall* before *The Creation* was finished at the first station. The Noah wagon, once it had ended its performance at the abbey, had to wait until the longer *Creation* had been played to the finish at the High Cross.

3. "The Staging of the Chester Cycle: An Alternate Theory," *Theatre Survey* 12 (November 1971): 119–50.

4. Harry N. Langdon, "Staging of the Ascension in the Chester Cycle," *Theatre Notebook* 26 (Winter 1971/72): 53–59, convincingly demonstrated that Christ could not have decorously ascended on a pageant wagon: "The use of cloud machines for ascensions either from high buildings or scaffolding seems more plausible."

The waiting period between the wagons got longer still for the spectators at the fourth or fifth stopping place. Thus there could be no "flow" of the action, and Rogers proves himself to be just as untrustworthy here as he was in his description of pageant wagons divided horizontally in two.

Powlick devised another solution of the problem. According to his assumption, the "pageants" indeed rolled through the streets, but did so only to take up their stations on the Roodee meadow at the end, where all the plays intended for a single day were performed. He called attention to the fact that in 1544 the mayor's proclamation of public peace was read on the Roodee meadow. Such an announcement outside the city walls, however, made sense only if the performances also took place there. Furthermore, Powlick discovered a reference to the River Dee and the city wall in the text: the river and the wall were visible to the spectators on the Roodee meadow; and the two city gates, of which the angel speaks in his warning to the Three Wise Men, could also be seen.

In opposition to Powlick, Ruth Brant Davis[5] has once again taken up the question of processions in Chester. See attempts to prove that the Chester Cycle was completely suited to a "stop-to-stop," and thus a "true-processional," manner of performance and made "an efficient schedule" possible. Her arguments have not convinced me. The lengths of the various "pageants" differ so much that there simply can be no regular progression of the pageant wagons. One more example of this may be adduced here: on the third day, *The Resurrection of Christ* had 527 verses, *The Ascension of Christ,* however, had only 192, and *The Last Judgment* closed the cycle with 708 verses. While Salter had discredited the *Breviarye,* ("there is hardly an accurate statement about the plays in it"), Davis is so devoted to Rogers that she even believes the *Breviarye* when the document speaks of pageant wagons divided horizontally into "higher and lower rooms." In the "lower rowme" Davis sees not only a place for changing costumes (as does Rogers) but also a sort of greenroom, where the actors rested in the pauses between performances, in that they evidently disappeared from the stage, the "higher rowme," into the lower region for a while. A highly unlikely hypothesis! If the pageants were to follow one another smoothly, as Davis has postulated, then the actors would have had no time at all for what she calls "relaxation."

Finally, mention should be made of a lawsuit (1568), for which there is documentary proof, between a Mr. Whytmore and a Mistress Webster, both of whom laid claim to the employment "of a mansion, Rowme, or Place for the Whydson plaies" in Bridgegate Street. Here some scholars saw a corroboration of their theory

---

5. "The Scheduling of the Chester Cycle Plays," *Theatre Notebook* 27 (1972/73): 49–67.

that spectators watched the processional performances of the Chester Cycle from the windows of the aforesaid house in Bridgegate Street. Nonetheless, Powlick had the idea that this case did not involve the renting of windows, but rather had to do with business interests of another sort, such as putting up vendors' stalls. Nelson[6] considered the possibility that the house in Bridgegate Street had a largish hall which was suitable for performances of plays from the Chester Cycle. Thus we have "indoor theater" instead of open-air performances. I regard this as the weakest solution of the mysterious legal dispute.

YORK

The manuscript, edited by L. T. Smith,[7] contains forty-eight plays. From the documents presented by Miss Smith we learn that in the year 1417 performances took place at twelve stops within the city; a grand total of sixteen stations was provided for in 1554, but in 1551 ten of them had been sufficient. On each occasion, the last performance took place on the "Pavement," a square which traditionally served as the place of judgment: here the accused were interrogated, tortured, and executed. The performances were limited to a single day. The actors, in full costume, had to be ready on their pageant wagons by 4:30 in the morning. Miss Smith did not worry about the practicalities of the processional form of performance which, she assumed, was followed here.

Much later, Martial Rose[8] questioned the actual possibility of giving a total performance of the cycle on a single day at ten to sixteen stopping places: "The processional street-pageant staging of the York cycle has been too readily accepted without due consideration of the practical problems." It was impossible to believe, he argued, that 13,121 verses could be spoken at ten, twelve, or sixteen successive stations on a single day. Even if the procession had started out at 4:30 in the morning, the last performance at the last station could not have taken place until long after midnight. In his calculations, Rose set the period of passage from one stop to another at only five minutes, and did not take the various lengths of the single plays into account, but rather worked with an "average" length of 273 verses. In fact, the first plays already show variations of 160, 86, 96, 99, and 175 in the number of verses. Thus, in York as in Chester, there was the same difficulty with the continuous movement of the procession. Furthermore, Rose brought up another question: why did all the actors

---

6. "Some Configurations of Staging," p. 131.
7. Lucy Toulain Smith, ed., *York Plays* (Oxford, 1885).
8. *The Wakefield Mystery Plays*, p. 24.

have to assemble at 4:30 in the morning when, for example, *The Last Judgment* did not begin its performance at the first station until 7:00 in the evening?

In a very useful study, Alan H. Nelson[9] went methodically to the heart of the matter. His calculations offered convincing proof that the York Cycle could not be performed on one day in a "true-processional" fashion. Forty-eight plays at twelve stops would have meant 576 performances on a single day. Even if the first performance took place at 5:00 in the morning, the last play could not have been performed at the final stop before 2:15 the next morning, provided, of course, that the wagons moved along, and followed one another, with uttermost precision. "The only method which would permit the cycle as it stands to begin and end between sunrise and sunset, even on a long June day, is a stationary, nonprocessional production so radically modified that it no longer conforms to the requirement that all plays should be seen at all stations in order."[10] Nelson proposed the following alternatives: the single plays were shortened; all the plays were not given at all the stops; the whole cycle was given at a single location, after the wagons had been drawn through the city. He opted for none of the possible solutions. Four years later, in his book,[11] he finally arrived at the opinion that the "pageants" did pass through the city as component parts of the procession, but that the spectators, lining the streets, did not get to see very much more than "brief actions," in other words, *tableaux vivants.* The cyclical performance itself was shifted by Nelson to an inside space, "the chamber of the Common Hall," where the mayor and the city fathers, stuffing themselves with food and drink, enjoyed the privilege of having the story of the Redemption acted out in their presence: the York Cycle in an "intimate theater," then, reduced to an amusement for a coterie. The York Realist surely never would have envisioned such a thing in his wildest dreams!

One of my students in the seminar for theatrical studies, David A. Kranes, presented a paper in 1966 in which he maintained that the theory of a processional performance in York is untenable, and that the performances of the cycle can only have taken place at a single spot, the so-called Pavement, York's place of judgment and market square. The dimensions of the square are twenty by one hundred yards. It extends from north-northeast to south-southwest; All Saints Church stands at the southwestern end, the parish church of Saint Crux is on the eastward side. For each of the forty-eight plays Kranes made an attempt to reconstruct a performance on the

9. "Principles of Processional Staging," *Modern Philology* 67 (1970): 303–20.

10. Ibid., p. 310.

11. Alan H. Nelson, *The Medieval English Stage, Corpus Christi Pageants and Plays* (Chicago, 1974), p. 78.

"Pavement." That the square is thoroughly suited for a polyscenic-stationary performance of the cycle is beyond question. Kranes did not exclude the possibility that
tableaux vivants were presented on the pageant wagons at designated points along
their way to the "Pavement." In this manner, the Pavement hypothesis could be
united with the documentary local notices from York, which expressly call for a
parade of the pageant wagons to follow a line of march through the narrow streets,
stopping before the houses of influential citizens.[12] To be sure, the documents say
that the "pageants shall be *played*" "against Harrison door," and "at Master Gate's
door." May we regard a tableau vivant as a mute "play"? Perhaps.

In 1415, Roger Burton, then town clerk of York, prepared an *Ordo paginarum
ludi Corporis Christi,* listing the cycle's pageants, the crafts assigned to perform them,
and the topics of each playlet. One of my students, Paul Sheren, wrestling with the
York problem in my seminar, made the observation that in some of his "plot" sum-
maries Burton seems to recall tableaux vivants he had seen in the procession. Take
Burton's description of the fifth pageant: "Adam and Eve with a tree between them.
The serpent tempting them with apples. God speaking to them and cursing the
serpent. An angel with a sword expelling them from Paradise." Clearly, this "scene"
could be mimed in front of spectators at every one of the designated ten to sixteen stations, and not much time would be lost. God's curse may have been the only crucial
lines actually spoken. Burton's comment on the eleventh pageant reads as follows:
"Moses raising the serpent of bronze in the desert. King Pharaoh, eight Jews in ad-
miration and expectancy." Sheren pointed out that the play did not call for eight
Jews. Only three Jews were required, the other characters were Egyptians. But who
among the watchers of a tableau vivant would be able to make this distinction as
long as the pantomime conveyed the feeling of awe evoked by the raised serpent?
Burton's "synopsis" of Play XXII has likewise charade character: "Jesus upon the
pinnacle of the Temple. The Devil tempting Him with stones. Two angels minister-
ing to Him, etc." Again an emblematic arrangement of parade figures that could
easily have been identified by the throng of spectators. Burton's reference to the
Entry into Jerusalem draws our attention once more: "Jesus upon an ass with its
foal. Twelve Apostles following Him. Six rich and six poor men, with eight boys
carrying palm branches, singing *Benedictus* etc., and Zaccheus climbing the sycamore
tree." The play has many more facets (the scene with the keeper of the ass, three
miracles) which Burton, evidently remembering a dumb show, ignored: Christ,

12. James F. Hoy, "The Staging Time of the York Cycle of Corpus Christi Plays," *The Emporia
State Research Studies* 21, no. 3 (Winter, 1973): 17, considered the possibility of fixed staging on the
Pavement but rejected the idea since "the records preponderantly rule for processional staging."

mounted on the ass, processionally enters Jerusalem, accompanied by a group of thirty-two followers. Our text calls for eight burgesses. But what Burton evidently saw was six men dressed to indicate affluence and six others costumed as paupers. Burton's condensation of Pageant XXXIV, the Bearing of the Cross, has likewise tableau character. However, it should be noted that the majority of Burton's action memos seem to be based not on visual memories but on his examination of the "orygynall." On the other hand, we should not dismiss, either in York's case or Wakefield's, the possibility of a *transitus figurarum* such as is certified for the Zerbst Corpus Christi celebration (see p. 70). An awareness of continental developments might be of benefit when we attempt to solve insular problems.

COVENTRY

I do not know of any attempt to transplant the Coventry Cycle from the streets of the city to a marketplace or a nearby meadow. For the rest, only two "pageants" from the cycle have come down to us, the play of the shearmen and tailors, and that of the weavers. The pageant of the shearmen and tailors has 900 verses (and three interlarded songs), that of the weavers is almost 1,200 verses long. It is characteristic of the Coventry plays—if we may draw any conclusions at all from the two surviving specimens—that, in contrast to Chester and York, they assign several biblical episodes to a single guild. Thus the guilds in Coventry were given a larger financial and moral burden than was the case in other English cities.

Hardin Craig[13] began by expressing the opinion that only ten "pageants" were provided for in Coventry. Later he did not exclude the possibility that Old Testament episodes were also incorporated into the cycle. But even if we keep only to the ten pageants with their average length of 1,000 verses, the performance at a single stopping point of the procession would have taken about ten hours; and so it hardly comes as a surprise that Queen Margaret, who had come incognito to Coventry in 1457 to watch the performance, could not see the last play in the cycle, *The Last Judgment,* "for lak of day," in other words, because it had become dark in the meantime. She was lodged, incidentally, at the house of the grocer Richard Woods: "there all the plays were furst pleyde," as we learn from the Coventry Leet Book. From this statement it becomes apparent that the cycle was repeated at another place, or perhaps at several places. The number of stopping points can no longer be determined.

When he published the two Coventry plays in 1902, Hardin Craig defended the

13. Hardin Craig, ed., *Two Coventry Corpus Christi Plays,* Early English Text Society, 13 (London, 1902), p. xiii.

thesis that the ten pageants of the cycle were performed at ten stations in the ten wards of the city. Half a century later, he was assailed by doubts concerning the feasibility of a tenfold cyclical performance: "ten stations seem too many."[14] Now, Craig weighed the possibility of only three cyclical performances on a single day. He supported this conjecture with an entry in the account books of the drapers. According to it, a sum of money was paid to one Mr. Crowe "for making of iij worldys." The drapers' play was *The Last Judgment,* in the course of which a globe was burned. Since in 1556 and 1558 mention is made of only three "worldys," Craig assumed that *Doomsday* was performed only three times, that is, at three stations, on a single day. But even a triple performance of the whole cycle of ten pageants is not feasible, again for reasons of time, "for lak of day." We are still waiting for other proposals —before Doomsday.

WAKEFIELD

When A. C. Cawley published his edition of the Wakefield pageants in the Towneley Cycle,[15] he also devoted a section of his work to the stage possibilities of these plays. Like others before him, he was inclined to believe that the Wakefield Cycle was performed "processionally."[16] Entries in the Wakefield Burgess Court Rolls of 1556 led him in this direction.[17] According to them, the members of the various guilds ("every crafte and occupacion") were required to have their pageant wagons ("bring furthe theire pagyaunts") in the procession on Corpus Christi Day, and, on the following holidays, "to gyve furthe the speches of the same," in other words, to play their roles. In addition, the document stipulated that every actor had to be at his wagon by 5:00 in the morning. Finally, the actors were instructed to perform only at the points agreed upon and nowhere else ("playe where setled and no where els"). It sounds quite similar to the York proclamation of 1415. Since Cawley proceeded from the assumption that the York plays were performed at single points in the city, he transferred this assumption to Wakefield, although further supporting documents do not exist in Wakefield's case. Cawley noticed, nonetheless, that in a number of the Wakefield plays there are spatial problems to be overcome, some-

14. *English Religious Drama,* p. 294.

15. *The Wakefield Pageants in the Towneley Cycle* (Manchester, 1958).

16. Ibid., p. xxv. In the course of a seminar sponsored by the Modern Language Association (Denver, December 1969) Professor Cawley pleaded for further study of pageant-wagon production. He saw in the currently faddish circular theater "a monstrously heavy machine which threatens to crush other medieval forms of theatre." See A. C. Cawley, "Pageant Wagon versus Juggernaut Car," *Research Opportunities in Renaissance Drama* 13/14 (1970/1971): 204–207.

17. *The Wakefield Pageants,* p. 124.

thing which then would require wagons of a great length. In my estimation, the mobile shepherds of the *Secunda Pastorum* would feel altogether trapped on a pageant wagon. In the introduction to his modernized edition of the cycle,[18] Martial Rose has raised the valid point that the arrival of the Three Wise Men cannot be dealt with on a pageant wagon, since the three kings come from three different directions on horseback, visit Herod, carry out the adoration of the infant in Bethlehem, go to sleep, and, admonished by an angel, once again ride away on their horses in three different directions. Rose refused to entertain the possibility of the processional manner of performance for Wakefield. The thirty-two extant plays have 12,276 verses. (Some episodes have been lost, so that the cycle may originally have contained as many as 15,000 verses.) From a practical standpoint it is impossible to perform a cycle of such dimensions more than once on a single day. This makes the processional form out of the question. Rose decides for a performance on three days in a poly-scenic-stationary form at a "fixed locality,"[19] perhaps of the sort for which we have evidence in the *Ludus Coventriae.* He postulates a more or less circular arrangement of the mansions on a square (before the church?) or a meadow with a nearby stone quarry. Cain asks that he be buried in "gudeboure at the quarrell hede." Goodybower is a meadow, in whose vicinity there was a quarry.[20] The neighborhood of a church is indicated by a verse in which Joseph of Arimathea suggests that the corpse of Christ be laid to rest in the "kyrke."[21] At any event, Rose has something in mind like the circular theater of the *Castle* or the arrangement of the mansions in Cornwall. Nevertheless, the Wakefield Cycle contains no references of any sort to a circular form. An arrangement of the mansions and the actors fronting toward the public ought rather to be taken into account—an arrangement such as we postulated for the *Ludus Coventriae.* As far as the directive quoted above is concerned, to the effect that actors must perform only at the places prescribed for them and nowhere else, it should not be read as a reference to the stopping places inside the city, by which the procession of tableaux vivants simply passed, but rather in connection with the place of performance, the square or the meadow, where the players—most likely during the rehearsals—were made to draw up their wagons at certain spots. Finally, to mention only one example, the mounted entrance of the Three Kings had to be worked out just as precisely, with respect to the spaces involved, in the case of the

18. *The Wakefield Mystery Plays,* p. 31.
19. Ibid., p. 30.
20. Craig, *English Religious Drama,* p. 208.
21. Nelson, *The Medieval English Stage,* p. 86. Nelson explores the Wakefield problems in greater depth in "The Wakefield Corpus Christi Play: Pageant Procession and Dramatic Cycle," *Research Opportunities in Renaissance Drama* 13/14 (1970/71): 221–33.

Wakefield rehearsals as in Lucerne under Cysat's direction. The whole problem of rehearsals is an unexplored and probably unexplorable aspect of the English cycles, although (since it involved amateur actors) it may not simply be shunted aside with a reference, say, to the role that tradition played and to the fact that parts frequently remained in the same hands.[22]

"THE CONVERSION OF SAINT PAUL"

The play is in the Digby Manuscript. The stage directions are extremely terse. All the same, we learn that Saul appeared in the guise of a noble knight, that a horse was placed at his disposal, that he fell from the horse, struck by the fiery light from heaven, and that the devils created a commotion with fire and thunder. But the *crux interpretum* lies elsewhere.

The play is divided into three parts, and each section is introduced by the Poet's prologue and concluded by an epilogue. In these passages we come upon some expressions which have led to varying interpretations of the manner of performance. At the end of the first part, the speaker of the epilogue, saying that one "stacion" is now finished, asks the public "to follow & succede ... thys generall processyon." The unbiased reader will immediately conclude that he is confronted by a processional play, especially since the Poet, in his introduction to the second part, remarks that "at thys pagent" the scene of Saul's conversion will be shown. Plainly, the spectators have marched in a procession with the poet to another station, where a new scenic configuration would be displayed, namely, "thys pagent." At the conclusion of the second part the poet ends "thys stacion," and then introduces the concluding section at a third point with the reference to "thys pagent at thys lytyll stacion." The public had reached the third point, once again in a procession. We learn nothing about the place of performance. A marketplace, a meadow, an intersection are possibilities. Opinions on the matter differ.

Before we let the various schools of thought speak their minds, we must direct our attention to the loca required for the play. After verse 140 Saul mounts his horse and "rydyth forth with hys servantes a-bowt the place & owt of the place." A short dialogue between Caiaphas and Annas ensues, bringing the first part to an end. By "place" we may probably understand an open square kept free of the audience, on which the stations for Saul, Caiaphas, and the stable were marked. Now, did Saul

---

22. Rose, *The Wakefield Mystery Plays*, p. 22. Martin Stevens, "The Staging of the Wakefield Plays," *Research Opportunities in Renaissance Drama* 11 (1968): 113–28, has offered certain corrections of Rose's theories.

ride ahead of the procession? In any event, he appears on horseback again at the opening of the second part, in which his conversion is accomplished. Saul is on the road to Damascus when he is cast from his horse and blinded by the bolt of heavenly lightning. A position for Deus was required ("Godhed spekyth in heuyn"), as well as stations for Ananias and for Saul (Ananias speaks of a "goodly mansyon"). For the third section, a place from which the devils make their entrance is needed and, moreover, loca for the high priests and for Paul, to whom an angel appears (from where?). Paul merely gives a report about the flight he plans to make from Damascus; the scene itself is not shown.

I do not hesitate to call the work a processional play, that is, I take the word *processyon* literally and regard the adjective *generall* as a reference to the spectators. We shall never find out at what distance from one another the three places of performance were located. The opinions about the manner of performance of this simple play are divided, nevertheless. One group of interpreters took the word *processyon* in its basic sense. Among these was F. J. Furnivall,[23] whose eye was caught by three "stations" distributed through a city; the spectators went from one to the next. Creizenach also observed that the Digby play of *The Conversion of Saint Paul* was calculated "to be performed in a procession."[24] Chambers likewise held fast to the procession theory: "The audience moved with the actors from one 'station' or 'pageant' to the other and back again."[25] To be sure, he had no very clear notion what this procession was like, since he imagined a platea with two loca (Jerusalem and Damascus), "with possibly a third for Heaven," as the place of performance. Thus he envisioned the two or three loca in considerable proximity to one another, so that the spectators only had to take a few steps to arrive at the next "station," from which they then returned to the first "pageant." For Chambers, *Saint Paul* was a play "for a small village." Craig thought perhaps of greater distances between "three separate playing-places," speculating that "the audience moves through a town or city in a sort of procession, a circumstance which suggests that in this play are still retained the features of the very earliest processional drama."[26] Martial Rose shows that he has been strongly influenced by Southern's circle scheme; since Paul rides "about the place and out of the place," Rose believes himself justified in proposing a staging in the round,[27] which would put the mansions on the periphery of a circular platea.

23. F. J. Furnivall, ed., *The Digby Mysteries* (London, 1882).
24. Wilhelm Creizenach, *Geschichte des neueren Dramas* (Halle, 1911), 1:304.
25. *The Mediaeval Stage*, 2:429.
26. *English Religious Drama*, p. 313.
27. *The Wakefield Mystery Plays*, p. 34.

Mary del Villar[28] has also rejected the idea of a procession. The Poet uses the word *processyon* only for the sake of the rhyme; his basic word is in fact *prosses* or *proces*, which has about the same meaning as "action." Del Villar has a notion of a "place-and-scaffolds mode of production," of the kind developed by Southern for *The Castle.* Nevertheless, if all the sedes had been arranged on or around a neutral "place," the action ("process") of the three sections would have gone along without any apparent breaks, and the Poet would have had no reason to introduce the second section with references to "thys pagent" and the third with "thys pagent at thys lytyll stacion." These references of the Poet had the direct function of making the spectators, who had been moving about in the pause between the sections, settle down and pay attention at this next stop of theirs.

Raymond J. Pentzell[29] could not reconcile himself to del Villar's theater-in-the-round. Returning to the procession, he perceived this technique of performance as a version of the medieval street theater. He was convinced that "three separate areas were defined by the three parts of the play."[30] A play in which the spectators themselves were movable appears to have been an unusual type of performance in England. Pentzell thought of the influence of the Franciscans, who—in England, as elsewhere—had developed an emotional-processional method for the adoration of the cross. However, del Villar was not to be shaken in her position; the theater-in-the-round had overwhelmed her.[31]

Glynne Wickham[32] sought another solution. Rejecting Furnivall's procession, he nevertheless borrowed two pageant wagons from him, wagons which Furnivall, in turn, had taken on loan from Thomas Sharp. Wickham's pageant wagons drew up on some marketplace or other before a public located in fixed seats. The marketplace was the platea. Wickham called the first pageant the Jerusalem wagon, on which Annas and Caiaphas were to be found. Saul emerged from a nearby inn, where the horse, which would be needed later, also stood waiting. Saul climbed from the platea onto the Jerusalem wagon, in order to receive the letters of the high priests. Then he descended from the wagon again and waited until the horse came. Next he rode away. Meanwhile Jerusalem was pushed to one side, making room for the second wagon, the Heaven wagon (with Christ and the angel) needed in the play's third

28. "The Staging of *The Conversion of Saint Paul*," *Theatre Notebook* 25 (1970/71): 64–68.
29. "The Medieval Theatre in the Streets," *Theatre Survey* 14 (May 1973): 1–21.
30. Raymond J. Pentzell, "Reply to Mary del Villar," *Theatre Survey* 14 (November 1973): 88.
31. Mary del Villar," "The Medieval Theatre in the Streets: A Rejoinder," *Theatre Survey* 14 (November 1973): 76–81.
32. "The Staging of Saint Plays in England," *The Medieval Drama,* ed. Sandro Sticca (Albany, 1972), pp. 99–119.

part. On Wickham's marketplace Damascus is indicated by cross-hatching. Sedes are not provided. Evidently, Ananias simply lounges around until Christ appears to him, encouraging him to baptize Saul. There is no trace in Wickham of the "goodly mansyon," where Saul is lost in religious contemplation. The play could doubtless be given in this form; Wickham may well offer proof of it in Bristol one day. In my estimation, though, we have not come any closer to the original manner of perform-ance. For the time being, we may choose from three theories: procession, theater-in-the-round, or pageant wagons.

THE PAGEANT WAGON DEBATE

Until recently, David Rogers's description in his *Breviarye* was regarded as a princi-pal source for the reconstruction of an English pageant wagon. The passage in Rogers runs: "these pagiantes or cariage was a highe place made like ahowse with ij rowmes beinge open on the tope the lower rowme they apparrelled & dressed them selues, and in the higher rowme they played, and they stoode vpon 6 wheeles...."[33] On the basis of this text, Thomas Sharp (1825) caused a pictorial representation to be made: it has subsequently refused to be eradicated from works on theatrical history. Sharp imagined a wagon of modest dimensions and with modest trappings. His "pageant" provides just enough space for a biblical episode, although the majority of the plays in the English cycles required several *loca ex opposito,* for which Sharp's wagon had no room at its disposal.

V. E. Albright[34] sought a solution by means of additional "scaffolds," put up at some distance from the main wagon, so that the actors made their way from one or another of the secondary wagons to the main wagon—for example, the shepherds in the fields went from their "scaffold" to the manger at Bethlehem, located on the main wagon. M. L. Spencer[35] refused to accept this theory: he wished to have all the man-sions or sedes needed in the play concentrated on a single wagon, something, to be sure, which would not have allowed the actors very much freedom of movement.

For his part, Glynne Wickham[36] imagines the existence of a "scaffold cart," which accompanied the main wagon. This "flat car," with no scenic elements, would have been shoved up next to the pageant wagon, so that the two of them together formed

---

33. Quoted from Harley MS 1944 by Salter, *Medieval Drama in Chester,* p. 56. Harley MS 1948 mentions only four wheels.
34. *The Shakespearean Stage,* p. 27.
35. *Corpus Christi Pageants in England* (New York, 1911).
36. *Early English Stages,* 1:173.

a larger area on which the action could unfold. Wickham was more or less compelled to search for an additional acting area of this sort: after all, he had expended a third of his main wagon on a (quite superfluous) "tiring house," closed off by curtains. In short, an extremely improbable solution. Such additional platforms can be proved to have existed in Spain, where they were required for the presentation of the "autos sacramentales" and were placed in city squares to await the arrival of the "carros." Nevertheless, they were not taken along in the procession proper, although the streets in Madrid or Seville would have offered more space for them than those in Chester or York.

Nelson accepts Wickham's additional wagon in principle, although he is aware of the technical difficulties which a second vehicle could cause in narrow streets. He imagines the "scaffolds" not to have been platform wagons but, instead, "large push-carts with two large wheels and one or two . . . caster wheels."[37] In my opinion, this theory also goes awry. I am inclined to assume that the term "scaffolds," found in some entries in the guild protocols, is not to be equated with "platforms," in Wickham's fashion;[38] rather, these "scaffolds" signify the mansions. In the *Ludus Coventriae* Herod sits in his "schaffalde," and Pilate, Annas, and Caiaphas in their "schaffaldys," that is, in their mansions. Thus, if an artisan was paid by the guilds for "setting and driving off the pagyn and skaffoldes," then we are confronted here with a pageant wagon ("pagyn"), on which the mansions ("skaffoldes") were erected; and if a worker received a sum of money "ffor mendynge of the skaffolds," these repairs refer to the mansions and not to Wickham's additional "scaffold cart."

M. James Young[39] refused to accept Wickham's assumption as common usage; nevertheless, he had to admit that the forty-eighth play in the York Cycle, *The Last Judgment,* could not be staged without a second wagon: a Heaven with nine inhabitants, a locus with three sedes for the judgment scene, a neutral area for the *animae,* and an elaborate Hell with three devils and two damned souls. Furthermore, the guild which was responsible for the play in 1472 entered in its book "nayls for both pagyants" and a payment "for bryngyng forth of the pagyantes into the strette."[40] Young would like to think that the two wagons were placed side by side, something for which the streets of York (twenty-five to thirty feet in breadth) were hardly suited. In the case of *The Adoration of the Three Kings,* Young also worked with two wagons, and, for *The Entrance into Jerusalem,* laid claim to both wagons and

37. *The Medieval English Stage,* p. 151.
38. *Early English Stages,* 1:171.
39. "The York Pageant Wagon," *Speech Monographs* 34 (March 1967): 1–20.
40. Ibid., p. 15.

street. For the remaining York plays, Young regarded a wagon with dimensions of ten to twenty feet as sufficient.

Since we possess no authentic medieval picture of a guild wagon, Hosley[41] adduced later pictorial documents, Denis van Alsloot's painting *The Triumph of Isabella* and William Boonen's engravings of the ten pageant wagons which were fitted out in Louvain (1594) for a procession in honor of the Virgin. It is reasonable to assume that van Alsloot achieved a realistic portrayal of the entry of the archduchess Isabella into Brussels (1615), even though the proportions can no longer be ascertained. Hosley estimated that the Brussels wagons had an average size of twelve by twenty feet; he worked out dimensions of ten by thirteen feet for the wagon with the tableau of the Annunciation. However, the wagon would be too small to allow the Annunciation scene from York to be played on it, because two mansions were required there, one for Mary and a second one for Elizabeth. In addition, the archangel had to appear and then to disappear again.

GERMAN CORPUS CHRISTI PLAYS

The German terminology speaks of "Fronleichnamsspiele" ("Corpus Christi plays"), "Prozessionsspiele" and "Umgangsspiele" ("processional plays") or "Bewegungsspiele" ("plays of movement"). In essence, these terms refer to mimetic performances which developed in connection with the Feast of Corpus Christi. Thus the expression "Corpus Christi play" is serviceable; "play of movement" is vague, leaving us in doubt about who—or what—is moving. The expression "processional play" is better suited to the various subordinate forms of these larger concepts. One of my students, Charles Swoope, has offered a precise definition of the situation with which we are confronted here: "By their very nature processional plays exist in a tension between pure play and pure procession. On the one hand, the requirements of staging dramatic episodes within a moving procession work against spoken drama and in favor of pantomime scenes as more suited for this type of performance condition. On the other hand, the desire to include spoken material tends to pull the processional play toward a fixed-stage production in which lengthy exchanges of dialogue could easily be accommodated." From this "tension" between procession and play there arise mixed forms of the sort which we still can readily detect in the Zerbst, Künzelsau, and Freiburg texts.

Wolfgang F. Michael coined the expression "Bewegungsspiel" ("play of move-

---

41. Richard Hosley, "Three Kinds of Outdoor Theatre before Shakespeare," *Theatre Survey* 12 (May 1971): 1–33.

ment"). The oldest German evidence of this form is provided by the so-called Innsbruck Corpus Christi Play, which cannot deny its descent from a still older *Processus prophetarum.* No fewer than twelve prophets foretell the birth of Christ, while the other monologues are put into the mouths of the Twelve Apostles, the Three Kings, Adam, Eve, John the Baptist, and the Pope. Creizenach could not find within the play itself any hints concerning the manner of its performance. Sepet was convinced that the play was performed during a procession. On the other hand, some scholars—Sengspiel and Dörrer among them—dismissed the connection with the Corpus Christi play. Brooks did the same thing: "It is a play of dogma and shows no connection with a procession."[42] For Michael, however, there was no doubt about the connection with the Corpus Christi procession, since various verses indicate that the holy wafer was visible during the procession. The connection with the procession is indeed undebatable; nevertheless, we are forced to take refuge in guesswork concerning the "technical" side of the performance, since the text, edited by Mone,[43] refuses to divulge any information when we put the following questions to it: In what city was the procession held? At what points was the march interrupted, in order to give the actors (who basically were costumed reciters of speeches) the chance to disclaim their didactic verses? It is precisely at this juncture that the appropriate archival material is missing.

In Zerbst we have the text for the performance of a Corpus Christi play in 1507, as well as documents referring to performances in the years 1511–22. The text of 1507 provides us with 399 rhymed couplets which indicate that the texts served to explain the tableaux vivants produced by the local guilds. W. Reupke[44] published a Latin document which determined the "order" of the procession for an undated performance. Thus we have solid evidence, for Zerbst, of the connection with the Corpus Christi procession. The single *figurae* were presented at the marketplace on which the procession made its first stop. Then the march continued to the Church of Saint Nikolaus, where the holy wafer was exposed on a "pallatium" during the "transitus figurarum." The performance consisted of tableaux vivants, which were explained to the faithful by a commentator. In addition, some biblical figures carried banderols, meant for those spectators who had good eyes and who could cope with the Latin (presumably members of the clergy, seated on benches in the immediate vicinity of the performance). For the rest, the costumes and properties were emblematic: the

42. Neil Brooks, "Processional Drama and Dramatic Procession in Germany in the Late Middle Ages," *Journal of English and Germanic Philology* 32 (1932): 167.

43. F. J. Mone, ed., *Altteutsche Schauspiele* (Quedlinburg, 1841), pp. 145–64.

44. Willm. Reupke, ed., *Das Zerbster Prozessionsspiel 1507* (Greifswald, 1930), pp. 18–22.

Adam-and-Eve *figura* was equipped with a tree and serpent, Moses bore the tablets with the Ten Commandments. The Slaughter of the Innocents was in a pronounced tableau-style: Herod, bearing crown and scepter and seated on his steed, was surrounded by vassals in armor, carrying lances on which the infants had been impaled; while four mothers, dressed in black, wrung their hands ("sollen sich stellen zu weynende"). The pantomimic element predominated. Should we not consider the possibility that, in the English mystery plays too, tableaux vivants of this sort—and nothing more—were presented at the separate stations of the cities? Such an assumption would solve a good many puzzles.

Of the German Corpus Christi plays, the one in Künzelsau has the greatest scope: its episodes range from the Creation to the Final Judgment. The connection with a procession is altogether visible, since each of the scenes was introduced by an explanatory statement of the "Rector Processionis," and the manuscript itself is entitled "Registrum processionis corporis christi." It divides the events of salvation into three sections with, respectively, nine, fourteen, and eighteen episodes, the majority of which are scenes with dialogue. Creizenach came to the conclusion that the three parts were performed at three points along the parade route on "stationary plank scaffolds."[45] We cannot agree with the editor of the play, Albert Schumann,[46] at all: he thought of a three-day performance on a meadow outside the city wall, calculating a total performance time of eleven hours. According to him, the actors were distributed on platforms arranged in rows, one platform to an episode, and the Rector and the spectators moved from one station to the next. Schumann's notion of a performance on the meadow can only be characterized as absurd.

Walther Müller took refuge in another hypothesis. He perceived no connection with a procession, thinking rather of a performance "in a church or in open space before the church."[47] He ignored the Registrum processionis, and "staged" the play in accordance with a Passion-play model à la Alsfeld. Brooks was quick to perceive the weakness of the supports on which Müller's thesis rested. When Müller wrote: "Hell, into which Herod and his daughter will be led, is already mentioned in the second part. Thus Hell was a permanent 'location' throughout the entire play, doubtless placed opposite Paradise, as was mostly the case in the passion plays and in pictorial representations,"[48] Brooks[49] was compelled to correct Müller's error: the Herod

45. *Geschichte des neuren Dramas,* 1:233.
46. *Das Künzelsauer Fronleichnamsspiel vom Jahr 1479* (Öhringen, 1926), pp. xviv–xvvi.
47. *Der schauspielerische Stil,* p. 101.
48. Ibid., pp. 101–02.
49. *"Processional Drama and Dramatic Procession,"* p. 164.

episode takes place in the third part, not the second, and a Hell is not needed at all before the harrowing, at which point a stage direction says, "Infernus preparetur." Dörrer[50] also speaks of a performance "in or before the church," but clings at the same time to "an extension of the play over three stationary localities."

Michael[51] reinstituted the connection with the procession. His assumption that the actors marched along with the procession appears reasonable. When the procession reached the initial station, religious functions were accomplished first of all. While the spiritual and lay dignitaries took their places upon seats reserved for them, the participants in the procession, together with the faithful who had awaited the procession's arrival at the station, remained standing as they followed the performance of the play's first part. The Rector introduced the individual episodes. The second part was performed at a second station, and the third at a third, while the parade fell into line again and again. The version which we possess (4,300 lines, without the additional 1,300) could be given in five hours. With its additional material, the play indicates a continuous growth of the cycle. We are not confronted here, as we are in the case of Innsbruck, with an original Corpus Christi play, but rather with a processional play which was well along the way to becoming a full-grown Passion play. The second scribe of the manuscript has thus redubbed the Rector processionis as "Rector ludi." While unequivocal proof exists for the participation of the guilds in Zerbst, the sources for Künzelsau are silent regarding the layer of the population from which the actors came.

A number of scholars have addressed their efforts to the Freiburg Corpus Christi Play (Sengspiel, Brooks, Michael, Dörrer). The extant archival material does not suffice for a valid reconstruction of the performance. The "ordnung des vmbgangs" of 1516 must serve as a basis; Brooks has provided its text.[52] From it we may obtain a clear view of the order in which the costumed groups appeared. The schoolmaster with cross and banner, followed by pupils crowned with wreaths, opened the procession—its mimetic part, at any rate. The painters' guild provided the first figura, represented by Adam and Eve "mit jr zůgehord," Cain and Abel. The coopers gave Abraham, Isaac, Joshua, and Caleb. Then the bakers followed with the "engelsch grůs." Next came the parish priest with his "liechtmess" group. The tailors were responsible for the Three Kings and their astronomer. The other guilds in the parade were as follows: the cobblers, tailors, carpenters, shoemakers, smiths, coopers, butchers,

---

50. In *Verfasserlexikon*, vol. 1, col. 773.
51. *Frühformen der deutschen Bühne*, p. 53. Also Brooks, "Processional Drama and Dramatic Procession," pp. 162–66.
52. "Processional Drama and "Dramatic Procession," p. 149.

goldsmiths, grocers, tanners, and vintners. It was no different than in York or Chester, save that there were no pageant wagons; in German territory, everything is "peripatetic."

We know that the procession began at the cathedral. The route through the city and the locations of the altar stations can no longer be determined. At any rate, the procession ended at the cathedral again. Our uncertainty extends to the following questions: What did the costumed groups present at the individual altar stations? Tableaux vivants? Brief dialogues? Were all the biblical episodes given at each station? Were verses recited as the procession went along? Was the total program performed only at the cathedral square and not before? The protocol book of the painters' guild, from which Michael provides excerpts,[53] contains a dialogue among the Devil, Eve, Adam, and an angel, barely forty lines of rhymed verse, which would completely lose its effect if it had to be spoken by the actors as they walked. This "play of movement" could thus only be unfolded at a halt in the procession. The first segment in the chain of episodes, it was no doubt already performed at the very first altar. Was it repeated at the second one, or was another "program" planned for that point? Michael deduced from the grievance petitions of the cathedral priest that the whole cycle was played at three stations.[54] Brooks arrived at the contrary opinion[55] that the Freiburg Corpus Christi Play was not given fragmentarily at single stations, but rather was finally produced in its totality at the cathedral square. Thus the "transitus figurarum" came first, and then, on the cathedral square, the "play"—at the outset in its simple form (1516), then expanded by the addition of the Crucifixion scene, and finally with Passion, Crucifixion, and burial. This development from "procession" to a Passion play might well have taken place in the last quarter of the sixteenth century. At this time we also hear of the construction of a "prügen," that is, a platform stage, and of stands for the spectators. The space between the "Kaufhaus" and the cathedral was ideally suited for this purpose.

53. "Die Anfänge des Theaters in Freiburg im Breisgau," *Zeitschrift des Freiburger Geschichtsvereins* 45 (1934): 72.
54. *Frühformen der deutschen Bühne*, p. 55.
55. "Processional Drama and Dramatic Procession," p. 155.

5 Pictorial Documentation

FOR THE PLAYS considered in the first chapter, we had only the rubrics at our disposal as we made our attempt to define the stage style. We now shall turn to French cycles for which pictorial evidence also appears to exist.

"THE MIRACLES OF NOTRE DAME"

In the Bibliotheque Nationale there is a manuscript collection of forty dramatized legends about the Virgin Mary, *Les Miracles de Nostre Dame par personnages*.[1] The manuscript was written at the end of the fourteenth century and ornamented with forty miniatures, one miniature to a play. The miracles of Mary issued from various anonymous hands and were performed in the assembly hall of the "puy des orfeures" [*sic*], that is, the Paris goldsmiths,[2] by lay actors in the years 1346–1380.

"Nous ne savon rien de la mise en scène de ces pièces," Petit de Julleville confessed.[3] In a chapter of his dissertation, Donald Clive Stuart[4] concerned himself with the manner in which the *Miracles* were staged, counting and cataloguing the mansions which the *puy* required for its cycle of miracles, without paying attention to the miniatures. Dorothy Penn[5] made the first serious effort to determine the stage form of these miracles. A second attempt at reconstruction comes from the hand of Robert Shiley.[6] In both investigations the miniatures were adduced in a manner implying that they contained the theatrical impressions of the artist. But the manuscript was prepared only after the conclusion of the series of performances—after 1380—and it is questionable whether or not the illuminator ever had the chance to see any of these performances at all; he may have only read the plays. In any event, the scenes which he presented seem to have been assigned to him by his employer. Rudolf Glutz has discovered in the manuscript "traces of instructions, written with silver

---

1. MS Cangé Nos. 819 and 820. The plays were edited by Gaston Paris and Ulysse Robert. 8 vols. (Paris, 1876–93).

2. Rudolf Glutz, *Miracles de Nostre Dame par personnages. Kritische Bibliographie und neue Studien zu Text, Entstehungszeit und Herkunft* (Berlin, 1954).

3. *Les Mystères*, 1:133.

4. *Stage Decoration in France in the Middle Ages* (New York, 1910).

5. *The Staging of the "Miracles de Nostre Dame par personnages" of Ms. Cangé* (New York, 1933).

6. In his unpublished dissertation, Yale University, 1939.

Miniature of the MS de Cangé no. 819 in the Bibliothèque Nationale, Paris, illustrating the eighth of *The Miracles of Notre Dame*. A wicked pope is kicked out of Saint Peter's in an unceremonious fashion. Our Lady with the Christ child evidently approves the eviction.

Miniature of the MS de Cangé no. 819 in the Bibliothèque Nationale, Paris, illustrating the eleventh of *The Miracles of Notre Dame*. A grove of trees, with the thief spying on a scene in which Our Lady is about to present a chaplet to the faithful merchant.

pencil, concerning the scene to be represented," directives for the "solid bourgeois artisan's art" of the painter.[7]

I can discover nothing in these miniatures which could be characterized as especially theatrical, that is, nothing which could be traced to impressions received from the stage. If the artist had been assigned the task of illustrating a collection of narrative legends, he would hardly have given his miniatures a form different from what they have here. The puy doubtless made use of the polyscenic stage of juxtaposition. This stage form, however, does not make its influence felt in the miniatures. Miniature number eight shows Saint Peter's Cathedral, but not the other mansions required for the play, such as the chapel of Our Lady, the palace of the pontifex, and the Heavenly Paradise. Thus we get only a partial aspect of the polyscenic arrangement. Number eleven is satisfied to show a clearing in the forest, although the play also demanded the house of a merchant and a hermitage. Miss Penn has come to the conclusion that thirteen mansions or loca are needed for number thirty-seven; but the miniature simply shows us the appearance of the white stag before Isabel and Anne, who, dressed in men's clothing, are sitting on their horses. Nary a trace of mansions is to be seen. Furthermore, at this juncture the play does not call for horses. Thus we have an unproductive miniature once again. From the texts we can learn that the puy, mindful that similar situations had to be repeated, maintained a number of pieces of movable scenery in its inventory: forest, mountain, hermit's cell, elevated Paradise, Hell, churches, cloisters, dwelling places, prison. The miniatures can only be of interest to scholars engaged in the study of costume: the dress is that of about 1400.

THE ARRAS PASSION

The miniatures adorning the manuscript of the so-called Arras Passion (around 1430, attributed to Eustache Mercadé) are likewise utterly unproductive for the theater historian. Petit de Julleville called for a careful investigation of these miniatures, "au point de vue de la mise en scène, dont elles pourraient éclaircir plus d'un détail obscur."[8] Jules-Marie Richard, the editor of the Passion, expressed doubts concerning the theatrical character of the miniatures (which were the work of four or five painters) when he wrote in his foreword: "Les miniaturistes ne se sont pas préoccupés du soin de nous donner la réprésentation du drame tel qu'ils l'avaient pu voir jouer dans quelque ville; ils ont traduit en images les rubriques de certaines scènes

7. *Kritische Bibliographie*, p. 205.
8. *Les Mystères*, 2:416.

de la 'Passion' et de la 'Vengeance', et parfois ils en ont fait d'agréables ou curieux tableaux."[9] Donald Clive Stuart has also warned against overestimating the miniatures, because the pictures do not agree with the stage directions.

Nonetheless, a number of these miniatures were published in various works on theater history. Cohen[10] reproduced twenty-eight of them, in fact, without making any statement about them, and Borcherdt offered eight of them,[11] again without any commentary. Let us examine Cohen's selection. The stall at Bethlehem appears in three variations, the first of them for the birth of Christ, then with some basic changes for the adoration of the shepherds, and then changed once again for the *officium stellae*. The circumcision scene has a gigantic Gothic cathedral as its background. Herod's learned men conduct their research in a well-equipped cloister library. The sickroom of Lazarus gives rise to a genuine little genre-picture, with a medicine cabinet and a cozy fireplace. The best to be said about these miniatures is that the artist has grasped the "spirit" of the various dramatic scenes. Thus, for example, Mary Magdalene's life as a whore, given a lively portrayal by Mercadé, is skillfully captured in a picture. The artists, quite gifted in part, followed iconographic models, the origins of which can no longer be determined in any detail. At any rate, it is meaningless to illustrate a theater history with such miniatures, for they give no information about the scenic form of the Passion, with its performance intended to be divided into four days. Instead of providing illumination, they simply confuse those minds which are all too eager to confound impressionism with scholarship.

"LA VENGEANCE DE NOTRE SEIGNEUR"

During the thirties of the last century, in the Reims cathedral, the municipal librarian Louis Paris discovered sketches for figured tapestries which he connected with the performance of the mystery play *La Vengeance de Notre Seigneur* at Reims (1531). He published these pictorial representations as engravings in the volume of plates included with his work *Toiles peintes*.[12] In addition, Paris employed three hundred pages to give a detailed analysis of the play, offering extensive textual samples from the edition of Jehan Petit.

La Vengeance is an anonymous cycle of about 22,000 verses, intended for a four-day performance. God's revenge against the Jews and the destruction of Jerusalem

---

9. *Le mystère de la Passion* (Arras, 1891), p. vi.

10. Gustave Cohen, *Le théâtre en France au moyen âge* (Paris, 1928), vol. I.

11. *Das europäische Theater.*

12. *Toiles peintes et tapisseries de la ville de Reims ou la mise en scène du théâtre des Confrères de la Passion* (Paris, 1843).

The counselors of Herod consulting their books. A miniature in the MS of the Arras Passion. Original in the Bibliothèque Municipale of Arras.

The illness of Lazarus. A miniature illustrating the MS of the Arras Passion. Original in the Bibliothèque Municipale, Arras.

were a popular anti-Semitic theme of the French Middle Ages. Eustache Mercadé, who died in 1440, is presumed to be the author of a manuscript *Vengeance,* which exerted a strong influence on our anonymous version. While Mercadé's play remained in manuscript, the anonymous *Vengeance* was made accessible to readers in several printings. There is documentary evidence for twelve performances of the mystère in various cities. The performance in Metz of 1437 aroused particular interest. For Metz we have a modest amount of archival information at our disposal;[13] for Reims only the faintest hints exist.[14] We know that the performance of the *Vengeance* followed a Passion play, that an entrance fee was charged, and that spectators who sat on the "échafauds" paid a lower price than the privileged folk who followed the play from windows.[15] No specific information is provided concerning the place of performance. Yet it appears reasonable to assume that we are dealing here with a public square in the city, surrounded by houses whose windows were rented out. Paris quotes a document in which the burghers propose to the city fathers that the play be given in the "lieu accoustumé." Georges Boussinesq and Gustave Laurent[16] have called attention to the fact that religious plays in Reims traditionally took place on the Place Coulture (today Drouet-d'Erlon). William E. Kleb, addressing himself to the problems of performance of the *Vengeance* in my seminar, found the Place Coulture to be "an interesting and tempting hypothesis," but added that caution should be exercised here.

It is tempting to seek answers to the many open questions by consulting the *toiles peintes* discovered by Paris. The sketches come from the time of the performance. The style of the costuming is "right": the early sixteenth century. Had the artist seen the performance of 1531 and then decided to immortalize his theatrical impressions on figured tapestries, or had he only read the play (there were printings aplenty) and given his imagination free rein? The artist may have seen the performance, afterwards doing with his impressions what he liked. A single question is of interest to the theater historian: can the pictures be used for a reconstruction of the performance, are they "credible"?

There is no doubt that they refer to the anonymous *Vengeance:* the choice of episodes and dramatis personae vouches for that. Besides, the first picture bears the inscription "Cy apres s'ensuit le mistere de la vengence de la mort et...Jesuchrist." The first toile shows scenes on the square before the Temple in Jerusalem. Musicians

13. L. Petit de Julleville, *Les Mystères,* 2:13.
14. Ibid., 2:117–19.
15. Louis Paris, *Le théâtre à Reims depuis le Romains jusqu'à nos jours* (Reims, 1885), p. 52.
16. *Histoire de Reims* (Reims, 1933), 1:382–83.

are playing. The Jews dance. The prophetic fool utters his warnings. Here we have "La bombance et dissolution des juifs et habitans de Jherusalem," as it says in the inscription. The picture could serve as a stage setting, with the Temple given a central location in the background and the individual mansions to the right and the left. The three towers, which are not required until the final day of performance, have already been set up. All of this could have offered itself to the gaze of the spectators on the marketplace in Reims in 1531. The second toile takes us to Spain, to the sickbed of leprous Vespasian, who is healed by the sudarium of Veronica. Where was this "Spain" located on the stage? Obviously, toile I gave us only a picturesque part of what was visible to the public. And where was "Rome" located for the scene between Tiberius and Pilate? Where was "Lyon," whither Pilate was brought by the devils? Paradise is not shown on the toiles at all. It is impossible for us to give it a specific location on the marketplace, nor do we know where the Hell stood from which, on occasion, the devils came swarming out. With toile IV the perspective undergoes a basic change. Now we are outside the city walls of Jerusalem. Toile I did not show any walls at all. Were these walls not put up until the third and fourth days of performance? In any case, the viewpoint in toile IV has shifted. Artistic liberties. Toile V returns us to the square before the Temple, but now the side toward the public is surrounded by a wall. Toile VI, the capture of the city, changes the perspective once more. Here it is patently the artist who is at work, not the recorder of a theatrical performance. Now, what do these pictures "accomplish" for theater history? Precious little. Again, they allow us to study costuming. Beyond that, they have no value. In his enthusiasm, which was no doubt fired by local patriotism, Louis Paris went too far, no question about it.

THE PASSION OF VALENCIENNES

When we proceed from the available pictorial material, as we have done in this chapter, the Passion performance of 1547 in Valenciennes appears to possess the best documentation. After all, the designer of the performance, Hubert Cailleau, had personally illuminated two Passion manuscripts,[17] thirty years after the event, to be sure. Assisted by Jacques des Moëlles, he seems in the frontispiece to have given a total view of the stage, which was erected in the courtyard and garden of the Hotel de Croy, the residence of the duc d'Arschot. And he did something more, in that he prefixed special miniatures for each of the twenty-five days of performance to the

17. Bibliothèque Nationale, MSS Fond français 12536 and Collection J. de Rothschild 1.7.3.

Engraving in Louis Paris's *Toiles peintes* (Paris, 1843) of presumed artist's impressions of a performance of the *Vengeance de Notre Seigneur* at Reims in 1531. The opening scene took place on the main square of Jerusalem.

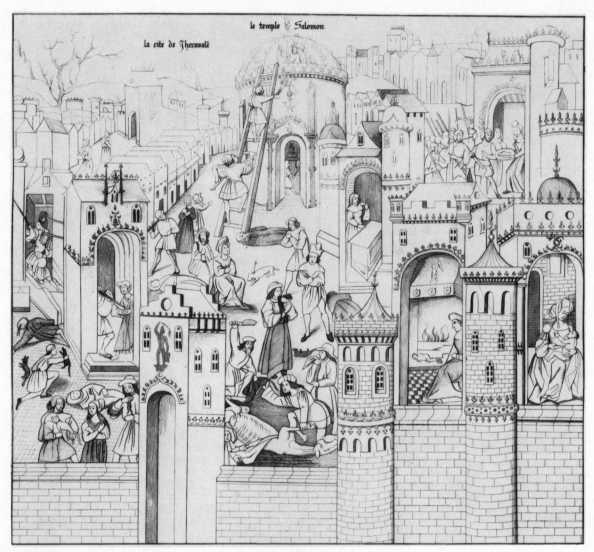

Jerusalem under siege. Artistic reflections of scenes from the *Vengeance de Notre Seigneur*, from Louis Paris's *Toiles peintes*.

The Passion play at Valenciennes (1547). Frontispiece of MS Rothschild, 1.7.3. in the Bibliothèque Nationale, Paris, executed by Hubert Cailleau and Jacques de Moëlles.

text, miniatures which were intended to call the mansions and the loca for the single days to mind.

As far as the frontispiece is concerned, Stuart long ago made the observation that Cailleau simply wished to paint an attractive picture here: "The miniature reproduces only a very small part of the scenery and is more or less fanciful."[18] Cohen conceived a simplified and stylized representation of the Valenciennes stage in the miniature: the frontispiece presented only the "decors fixes," while further scenic elements were adduced in the course of the performance, "quelques practicables et décors mobiles, installés par les machinistes quand besoin était."[19] He estimated that about seventy "lieux" were needed for the Passion, while, he said, the title page showed only twelve. Furthermore, in the employment of additional pieces of movable scenery, Cohen found "un élément de successif,"[20] which, he believed, looked into the future, announcing the beginning of the end for the principle of simultaneity. I cannot agree with him on this point. The use of additional pieces of movable scenery does not mean an abandonment of the polyscenic principle, but a strengthening of it instead.

A ground plan of the Hotel de Croy has yet to be discovered.[21] Elie Konigson made some guesses about the dimensions of the stage. According to his estimates, the stage was 58 meters long and 17.50 meters deep.[22] Konigson himself called these figures "dimensions hypothétiques"; his calculations are based on certain dimensions of height, about which our sources contain a few hints. Otherwise, the archival material, however rich it is, merely reveals to us certain details concerning organization. We possess but one sure fact: the public stood (for six deniers in the parterre) or sat (for twelve deniers "sur ung hordement") in front of a rectangular platform. If the various miniatures are intended to help us with the distribution of the mansions, they are altogether misleading. As befits miniatures, these are infused with so many picturesque elements (such as perspective views and effects of depth) that we may present them as theatrical evidence only on a limited scale.

Despite these restrictions, Elie Konigson had the courage to undertake a reconstruction of the performance, believing he could find support for his work in the rubrics and miniatures. He divided the stage platform into three sections, proceeding

18. *Stage Decoration in France,* pp. 108–09.
19. *Le livre de conduite,* p. lxxxvii.
20. *Etudes d'histoire du théâtre,* p. 235.
21. Rey-Flaud, *Le cercle magique,* pp. 218–22, attempted to identify the site of the Valenciennes performance, but the maps on which he relied offer hardly conclusive evidence.
22. *La représentation d'un mystère de la Passion à Valenciennes en 1547* (Paris, 1969), p. 51. Rey-Flaud, *Le cercle magique,* p. 221, questions Konigson's measurements; he assumes an acting area of 16 by 18 meters, a stage, moreover, which he places in the center of the auditorium.

from the assumption that the distribution of the mansions on the frontispiece was preserved basically unchanged throughout the whole performance, thus on all twenty-five days. To be sure, Konigson noticed the absence of the mountain, which had various functions to fulfill in the course of the cycle, from the frontispiece. He placed this mountain on the enclosed plain before the gate of Nazareth. Since Heaven and Hell were in daily use, we may assume that these two mansions had a permanent location for the duration of the performance, a location determined by Cailleau. The identity of the Temple—although not its position under every circumstance—was maintained throughout the cycle. I am also willing to follow Konigson's conjecture that the mansion denoted as "salle" was a neutral location, taking its identity in accordance with events. The palace remained a palace. For the rest, I believe that Konigson was almost hypnotized by the frontispiece, which shows an arrangement of the mansions in a manner not required on any of the twenty-five days of performance. Each day demanded a fresh orientation between Heaven and Hell.

Examining Konigson's "strategic" ground plans, one is struck by the fact that the left side of the stage is favored and that, if one is willing to follow his entries on the sketches, it often happens that no important action takes place on the right half of the stage for days at a time, apart from the *diableries*. Konigson not only crams the mountain into the space between the "salle" and the Temple, but also the Nativity scene, of which he has a simpler conception, by the way, than that painted by Cailleau for the fourth day. The Mount of Olives and the scene of the Transfiguration are also moved into the neighborhood of Paradise, since it makes the appearance of angels easier. But as Konigson himself pointed out, flights over the whole length of the stage could be arranged in Valenciennes (and elsewhere). The rigid frontispiece scheme seduced Konigson into arriving at quite untheatrical solutions. I should like to assume that, in his eighth miniature, Cailleau depicted a stage event when he portrayed the son of the king of Iscariot playing chess with Judas in a mansion. Removing the mansion, Konigson has the episode played in a corner to the right of the Golden Gate. Since at this point, behind the "mer," the frontispiece does not show a mansion, Konigson has also failed to take a mansion into account. A building in the back wall is denoted in the frontispiece as a "maison des évèques." In opposition to Konigson, I should prefer, all the same, not to assume that the scenes with Annas and Caiaphas were played—once again—behind the "mer." The scene in which the man sick with palsy is lowered on a bier through the opened roof to Christ is likewise banished by Konigson to the space behind the "mer," since there, in the wall next to Limbo, he detects a house sketched in. It is inconceivable that this scene, rendered by Cailleau in his tenth individual miniature, was simply shoved into a corner by the director.

The cure of Peter's mother-in-law (on the ninth day) takes place, in Konigson's version, someplace in the middle section of the stage. Nevertheless, the miniature shows how Christ visits the sick woman in the house of Peter. Konigson has not provided a mansion in this instance, either. He refuses to allow himself any flexibility. Nonetheless, I suggest that the arrangement of the mansions underwent changes from one day to the next, and that additional mansions were included as the events called for them. I could imagine, for example, that on days when the "mer" was not needed, the "surface of the water" (sheep skins dyed blue?) was covered with boards, in order to create additional room for pieces of scenery and for possible developments of the action.

6 Pictorial Art or Theater?

"PRIMO LE PAROLE, DOPO LA MUSICA." . . . The feud between the followers of Piccini and Gluck, which stirred the hearts and minds of Paris once upon a time, subsided quickly; today it leads only a gentle afterlife in *Capriccio,* with its masterly orchestration. For a century now in the discussion of medieval religious theater and pictorial art, the question of *primo/dopo* has been a matter of concern to the world of scholars, to the historians of art and theater alike.

MÂLE: THE PRO AND THE CONTRA

Three theses were taken up in the course of the controversy:

1. Pictorial art borrows iconographic motifs from the religious drama, in which process the drama must be granted priority: P. Weber, K. Tscheuschner, E. Mâle, G. Cohen, G. Frank, A. Rohde, A. Rapp, W. L. Hildburgh, and M. D. Anderson are among the parties involved—to name only a few of the most valiant.

2 Art and theater draw upon common literary and, for the most part, noncanonical sources, whether they be the Gospel of Nicodemus, Pseudo-Bonaventure, the Golden Legend, or mystic sermon-literature. According to this thesis, we are confronted with developments in art and in the theater which were parallel, even though by no means synchronized. Thus spake Ernst Grube: "The religious plays are a parallel phenomenon, coming later in time, to the same development in pictorial art. An influence on pictorial art by the mystery plays cannot be considered."[1]

3. With traditions going back to Byzantium, graphic art has temporal precedence and exerts an influence on the mystery plays: W. Pinder, A. D. Sensenbach,[2] F. P. Pickering.[3]

Grube has followed the course of the debate chronologically. From his sketch it emerges that Mâle wrought the worst mischief: coming from modest predecessors, he begat a large and immodest progeny. Grube and Sensenbach do not diverge in demonstrating the absurdity of Mâle's assertions; each of them simply stresses somewhat different factors. Sensenbach also hales English scholarship into court—Hild-

---

1. "Die abendländisch-christliche Kunst des Mittelalters und das geistliche Schauspiel der Kirche," *Maske und Kothurn* 3 (1957): 57.
2. Sensenbach, one of my former students, presented the results of his research in an unpublished dissertation, Yale University, 1965.
3. *Literatur und darstellende Kunst im Mittelalter* (Berlin, 1966).

burgh, for example—and puts a special emphasis on Byzantine art, of which Mâle had taken no notice. In an "excursus," Grube likewise refers to Byzantium as an iconographic source for pictorial art, but in specific cases makes the mystical movement responsible for the appearance of certain motifs in pictorial and in stage art.

Mâle asked the following question: How did it come to pass that in the course of the fifteenth century iconographic innovations swept through pictorial art, that artists became interested in new motifs or at least imbued old ones with a strong realism, and that stylized and sentimentally sweet elements were crowded out by "reality"? His answer went: "ce changement s'explique par l'épanouissement du théâtre religieux dans la chrétienté tout entière au commencement du XVe siècle."[4] After he had made the religious theater responsible for the change of style in the graphic arts, Mâle sought a reason for the change of religious theater's own style. He traced this change back to the growing reputation of the *Meditationes*. Friar John had emotionalized, humanized, essentially "dramatized" the narrative material present in the New Testament, erecting veritable edifices of sentimental emotionalism, as in the departure of Jesus from his mother. The dramatists seized greedily upon the pious dreams of the mystic. As Mâle expressed it with a primo/dopo, the new material was acted first and painted only afterward.[5] Mâle must have proceeded from the assumption that the painters could not read, having to depend on the theater as a kind of *Biblia Pauperum* in order to garner stimulation for their paintings. When we pursue Mâle's commentary in a single detail (and it is always a question of details and nothing more), we get a plain view of the grotesque distortions to which such an assumption can lead. The *Meditationes* tell how Mary leaned against a column in the manger at Bethlehem during the delivery of the Christ child. A column also supports the roof in the nativity scene of Rogier van der Weyden. In Hugo van der Goes the column is sturdier still. Nor can Memling get along without it. From this circumstance Mâle draws a remarkable conclusion—not that the painters have read the *Meditationes* but that they had seen a similar column as a stage property at performances of *Mystères flamands,* now lost. The *Meditationes* tell of a visit of the Holy Family to Elizabeth, during which the Christ child and the boy John played with one another, a scene which inspired Raphael and second-line painters as well. Since he could find no dramatic counterpart for this, Mâle had to admit that the scene was simply borrowed from the *Meditationes* by the painters, without any connecting link in the theater.

4. Émile Mâle, "Le renouvellement de l'art par les 'Mystères' à la fin du Moyen Age," *Gazette des Beaux-Arts* 31 (1904): 96.
5. Ibid., p. 216: "Ils [the artists] peignaient donc ce qu'ils avaient vu."

Mâle attributed the realistic harshness with which the events of the Crucifixion forced their way into pictorial art around 1400 to the beginning of Passion performances in Paris at this time. Here, Grube referred to the decisive influence of mystic literature: "All the motifs which appear in this connection, especially those concerning the depiction of the Redeemer's pain and anguish, are already present in the writings of the mystics, and come from this source into pictorial art."[6] Grube called attention to Master Bertram's nailing of Christ to the cross: at the end of the fourteenth century, thus before the Parisian Confrèrie had received its license, he painted a bluntly realistic representation of the Crucifixion (complete with stretching of ropes and hammering of nails) as an altarpiece.

Mâle summarized his ideas at the end of his series of essays: "Les tableaux, les vitraux, les miniatures, les retables nous offrent sans cesse l'image exact de ce qu'on voyait au théâtre. Certaines oeuvres d'art sont des copies plus frappantes encore, car l'action y est simultanée, comme dans les Mystères. Les Tableaux de Memling consacrés à la Passion et à la vie de la Vierge—où l'on voit dix scènes différentes se derouler sur la même fond de paysage, où les acteurs du drame se transportent naïvement d'une mansion à une autre,—nous donnent l'idée la plus exacte d'une représentation dramatique."[7] Gustave Cohen, who confessed that he was wholly of Mâle's faith, likewise mentioned Memling's *Passion,* making the assertion "que les plus grands artistes ont emprunté aux Mystères le décor simultané."[8] But an objection must be raised against such visionary notions, for in Memling's *Passion* we have no "extremely exact" representation of some theatrical performance or other before us, just as we may not trace the *Bayeux Tapestry* back to a lost play depicting the Norman Conquest. In the tapestry, as in Memling's painting and the miniature mentioned by Cohen (with its juxtaposition of the annunciation made to the shepherds and their adoration of the Infant), a story is told in a Gothic fashion, and the viewer is invited to read off in succession the delineated episodes of a mute drama. Here we are not confronted with influences but with the Gothic period's practice of successive presentation, held in common by both art and theater. Memling's *Passion* is useless as a document for theater history. The picture remains a work of art, of Gothic expressionism. A medieval artist has presented us with a documentary theatrical picture only once: Fouquet in his miniature of the torture of Saint Apollonia. Otherwise, we owe documentary material merely to third-rate painters or draftsmen: Cailleau Raber, Cysat.

6. "Die abendländisch-christliche Kunst," p. 57.
7. "Le renouvellement de l'art," p. 390.
8. *Histoire de la mise en scène,* p. 113.

In a Frankfurt lecture (1917), Julius Petersen registered a divided attitude toward Mâle. Of the Gothic painter he said: "He painted what he saw. The holy events actually moved through the streets of the Low German city just as they do in the pictures of Hans Memling."[9] In other words: an influence of the theater on pictorial art. "On the other hand, the staging of the play could only be enriched by pictorial examples."[10] Primo? Dopo? And finally Petersen's pertinent observation, illuminating the irrelevance of all these efforts: "Art gave itself over to the suffering of Christ in a more impassioned empathy than the mechanical naturalism of the theatrical embodiment allowed. ... In art the living force of a strong personality burst forth. Pictorial art gave its best where it liberated itself from the conventions of the theater."[11] Max Hermann had already rejected the thesis of H. Kehrer,[12] according to which the plays about the Three Kings had influenced French painting: in the case of gestures for which evidence of both a pictorial and theatrical nature exists, Hermann maintained, the question need not be that of a direct connection, "but rather both arts can have arrived at the same conclusion independently of one another."[13]

In an important essay, Wilhelm Pinder[14] freed the pictorial representation of the Pietà motif from any dependency on the theater. The fertilizing element for representations of the Pietà (vesper pictures, works of plastic art) did not come from the stage, nor from dramatic Marian laments, but from lyric monologues which go back to the twelfth century. "The roots of the Pietà are lyrical. The artists who first gave the subject plastic form (many factors argue for their having been Germans) translated a poetic dream which, maturing in verbal form, had grown steadily over a period of centuries in the direction of visible art. They did not reproduce a view of a theatrical scene; instead, prior to the stage, they truly translated the emotionalism— molded in words—of originally lyric conceptions."[15] These were the steps of the development: lyric, epic, and pictorial, "and only then does the director of the religious play follow at a distance."[16] It comes as no surprise that Pinder was skeptical toward Mâle's "influences" and did not know what to make of Cohen's Histoire.

9. Das deutsche Nationaltheater, p. 15.
10. Ibid.
11. Ibid., p. 16.
12. Die heiligen drei Könige in Literatur und Kunst (Leipzig, 1908).
13. Max Hermann, Forschungen zur deutschen Theatergeschichte des Mittelalters und der Renaissance (Berlin, 1914), p. 241.
14. "Die dichterische Wurzel der Pietà," Repertorium für Kunstwissenschaft 42 (1920): 145–63.
15. Ibid., p. 161.
16. Ibid., p. 163.

F. P. Pickering, who was especially concerned with the representation of the Crucifixion entertains a similar skepticism toward Mâle's hypotheses: "it may be also asked if the mystery plays, which cannot have introduced a *renouvellement* of art in the sense of Mâle's early thesis, are to be completely left out of account in the future. For various reasons I believe their influence was probably slight.... The painters did not paint their scenes the way they had seen them in the drama; instead, they followed the directions provided in the biblical *sicut-ita* formulas."[17] Pickering believes in influences from common textual sources (Pseudo-Anselm, Pseudo-Bonaventure), on which both painters and dramatists drew: "It is simply no longer possible to reconstruct the history of medieval crucifixion iconography on the basis of thoughts about what one could expect from a medieval actor."[18] Pickering reckons with an influence of pictorial art on the theater: "the picture of the artist provided [the director] with a mirror; he very likely referred to the artist's picture when he wanted to instil some discipline into his troupe."[19]

In the field of Italian theatrical scholarship, new land has been discovered by Virginia Galante Garrone,[20] in particular with her reconstruction of the performance style of the Umbrian *laude.* She has proved that the central piece of scenery of the *Disciplinati* was the mountain, *il monte,* which, as such, in a solid form or hollowed out (*caverna, grotta*) dominated the stage of the Umbrian tabernacles. The *didascaliae* of the various collections of laude point again and again to the presence of a mountain as the center of the holy action. We also meet the mountain motif in pictorial art. Galante Garrone does not believe in an influence exercised by the stage: "io ammetto più facile e più diretta una dipendanza degli allestitori scenici dagli artisti benchè il Mâle pensi il contrario."[21] But here too it is evidently a question not of a mechanical "rapporto" but of a common creative urge ("uno stesso impulso formale"), which was decisive in giving pictorial and theatrical art their conformation. Nevertheless, the author emphasizes the primacy of pictorial art: "è molto probabile che alla scena la rivelazione delle possibilità formali e plastiche di un monte sia venuta dall' arte figurativa."[22] For the central position of il monte, at any rate, there exists pictorial evidence from a hundred years before the Disciplinati staged their laude.

17. *Literatur und darstellende Kunst,* p. 109.
18. Ibid., p. 108.
19. Ibid., p. 110.
20. *L'Apparato scenico del dramma sacro in Italia* (Torino 1935).
21. Ibid., p. 21.
22. Ibid., p. 80.

ENGLISH SURMISES

W. L. Hildburgh is regarded as an authority on English alabaster, a subject to which he has devoted a series of essays; in these alabaster carvings he sees folk art produced by more or less gifted craftsmen. In a lecture of 1939,[23] he tracked down the connections between art image and stage, proceeding in a decidedly more cautious manner than had Mâle. Several times he weighed the possibility of parallel phenomena arising on the basis of common literary sources. Hildburgh got his theatrical information from the rubrics of the English mystery plays. By means of his alabaster studies he hoped to attain a more exact idea concerning the performances of these guild cycles. The results, to be sure, were very slight, and our knowledge of the processional style of performance was by no means enriched. When on an alabaster tablet, "The Purification of Mary," a priest is shown standing under a Gothic arch, we can hardly share Hildburgh's optimism: he is inclined to the assumption that "the arched opening...depicts fairly accurately a type of stage property used regularly to represent almost any kind of edifice wanted for the action."[24] "Mary's Visit to the Temple," on another tablet, appears to the unbiased observer to be merely an unsuccessful try at giving a pictorial representation of the three-year-old girl's ascent of a great many stairs. It would be fruitless to do what Hildburgh has done—to transfer the unhappy perspective onto a pageant wagon. Now and then the notion of a "stage influence" turns out to be farfetched indeed. On yet another alabaster tablet, "The Mocking of Jesus," Christ is struck on his head with clubs. One of the clubs is bent. Hildburgh's opinion is this: we are confronted with a theatrical prop, actually nothing more than a long stuffed sausage, which could not do any damage to the actor playing the role of Christ. In two cases, alabaster tablets with *hortulanus* scenes have their foregrounds delimited by a low wooden fence. Once again, an impression gained from the stage is made to bear the responsibility. The stylized garden on the tablet of the duke of Rutland is also regarded as a copy of a stage garden. When Hildburgh calls attention to the fact that an alabaster Pilate washes his hands while a servant holds out a basin of water for him, the presence of the servant again is traced to impressions from the mystery plays. The figure of the servant, however, has a long iconographic history: it already appears on sarcophagi of the fourth century, and on Byzantine mosaics as well. In England itself, a servant hands Pilate the basin in a miniature of the Albani psalter from the twelfth century, thus long before play-acting ever entered the heads of the honest guild members.

23. "English Alabaster Carvings as Records of the Medieval Religious Drama," *Archaeologia* 43 (1949):52–101.
24. Ibid., p. 72.

M. D. Anderson[25] chided Hildburgh for having limited himself to works in ala-baster, ignoring murals, glass paintings, and wood carvings. In her book, therefore, Miss Anderson was particularly keen in her pursuit of the connections between drama and pictorial art as they may have appeared in the works of glass painters and woodcarvers. A hunt for parallels is begun in which nondramatic literary creations are not declared out-of-bounds as possible common sources. The author grants that a good many of her assertions are basically nothing more than surmises, even though she would like to make a strong claim for the probability of others. Nevertheless, her surmises and her probabilities come to an end when, in her seventh chapter, she settles down in Norwich cathedral to study the iconography of the wood carvings in the vault of the transept, intending—on the basis of this research—to call the lost dramatic cycle of Norwich back to life. She is convinced "that the carvers of the transept bosses in Norwich Cathedral did something which is unique in British imagery, and, so far as I know, unparalleled in European art, they left us a detailed impression of some plays they had seen, and it is much more likely that they were remembering the Norwich Cycle than that of any other city."[26]

The Norwich Cycle has been lost. Only the melancholy fragment of a *Fall of Man* remains, together with a list of the plays comprising the cycle in 1527, when the members of the Guild of Saint Luke made it clear to the city fathers that the guild was no longer financially able to bear the burden of the cycle's production. Of the twelve episodes named in the guild list, eight derived from the Old Testament. Number Nine dealt with the birth of Christ (with shepherds and the Three Kings). The baptism of Christ followed. No scenes from the Passion were provided for at all. The cycle ended with the Resurrection and the miracle of Whitsuntide.

The 150 carvings in the vault of the Norwich transept are from 1509, when the cathedral was restored after a fire. From the themes treated by the carvers, Miss Anderson arrives at the scenes that had found a place in the original Norwich Cycle, a cycle which, accordingly, contained scenes starting with the birth of John the Baptist and ending with the cure of Peter's mother-in-law. What have we achieved in the process? At the best, a reference to a vanished literary document. For there can be no question of a performance reconstruction, made with the aid of the carvings, which could satisfy a theater historian. The carvings which Miss Anderson analyzes with pious curiosity are too crude to provide any information about the style of per-formance. In the event that the carvers did indeed employ theatrical impressions (something which was altogether possible), then we learn that Joseph appeared as

25. *Drama and Imagery in English Medieval Churches* (Cambridge, 1963).
26. Ibid., p. 87.

a bearded man, that Herod was indicated by a crown, that John wore a garment of skins, that the scribes were supplied with capes of ermine, and that the archangel Gabriel appeared in a remarkable costume: bare legs, and a tight corset with large wings. Otherwise, we are no better off than we were before. Miss Anderson closes her Norwich chapter with the following reflection: "It is important to remember always that it was never the intention of medieval craftsmen to record plays as such, but when called upon to represent the same subjects which they had seen acted, these stage scenes were literally copied by unimaginative carvers."[27] Alan H. Nelson,[28] who has endeavored to make a reconstruction of the lost cycle, thinks it likely that the plays were not performed processionally, but rather were given a stationary per-formance in an open field; Chapel Field or Tombland would be possibilities. I men-tion this only in passing.

In an important study,[29] Otto Pächt has investigated the entrance of the "continu-ous method" into English miniatures, asking himself the following question among others: How did it happen that a "pictorial narrative" developed out of an Emmaus scene with a unity of space and time (Christ sitting at a table between two pil-grims)? In miniatures, first of all, the scene is shown in which the two pilgrims meet the Savior, whom they do not recognize. The two pilgrims then call attention to the fact that the day is coming to an end; the three of them sit down to eat, and the pilgrims finally remain there without Christ, who has removed himself from their gaze in some mysterious way. In answering the above question, Pächt adduces rubrics from various liturgical *peregrini*-dramas (they can be looked up in Karl Young), for he is completely convinced of the priority of "the dramatized version that was the starting point for the English twelfth-century illuminators."[30] It could be rejoined that the dramatic mode of representation was inspired by the "narrative" in the Gospel of Saint Luke, and that it is impossible to see why the same canonical report could not also have fired the imagination of the miniature-painter. The artist of the miniatures in the Albani psalter has the pilgrims call attention to the approach of evening by depicting the slantwise rays of the sun. This is a purely pictorial means of doing justice to the "inclinata est iam dies" of the Gospel. The sunset was cer-tainly not shown on the contemporary "stage." In the same psalter the artist has represented the "ipse evanuit ex oculis" as an ascension: only the feet of the Savior are still visible as he floats away. Once again a painter's solution of the problem,

27. Ibid., p. 103.
28. *The Medieval English Stage*, pp. 119–37.
29. *The Rise of Pictorial Narrative in Twelfth-Century England* (Oxford, 1962).
30. Ibid., p. 41.

for the liturgical dramatist surely had no flying machine at his disposal. In the rubrics it merely says, in a quite unpictorial way, "subito recedens" or "latenter discedet," whereupon the actor playing the role of Christ simply disappeared behind a curtain.

THE ROLLINGER CASE

The golden age of the Viennese Passion Play falls in the years 1505–1512, when two vigorous personalities, Matheus Heuberger, a well-to-do burgher, and the wood-carver Wilhelm Rollinger had the administration of the Brotherhood of the Body of the Lord ("Gottsleichnamsbruderschaft") in their charge. During these years, and beyond, the Brotherhood bore the responsibility for outfitting the Corpus Christi procession and for the theatrical performances connected with it.

The Viennese Passion Play has not come down to us. Its style of performance was stationary in part, and in part processional street theater. To the extent that we can deduce the nature of its contents, it consisted of two sections connected by a processional transition. The first part, which was played on the New Market ("Neuer Markt"), concerned the preamble of the Passion up to the time when Christ is taken prisoner. The Crucifixion and the entombment took place on the "Freithof" of Saint Stephan's or in the Tirna Chapel. In between lay the "parading" ("Ausführung") of Christ, in other words, the way of the cross, in the form of a procession ("Umgang") which took actors and spectators through the streets of Vienna from the New Market to the Cathedral of Saint Stephan. Annas and Caiaphas rode on horseback. Christ fell beneath the weight of the cross. Simon of Cyrene came to his aid. Veronica gave Christ the sudarium. It can no longer be decided if these scenes were presented as tableaux vivants or if, instead, there were spoken texts. Originally, the play was performed on Corpus Christi Day in connection with the procession and moved to Trinity Sunday, in order to avoid overburdening all the participants. The "Regierer" (director) of the performances was Rollinger.

Maria Capra[31] has culled these details of organization from the "Raitbücher" (account books) of the Brotherhood. The archival springs flow abundantly as long as we ask them for information about costumes and properties. To be sure, we learn nothing about the appearance of the mansions. There is documentary evidence for the erection of four "pun," (platforms) on the New Market in 1505. From an inventory of the Brotherhood we learn that it possessed an "Ölperg, so man am Newenmarkht gepraucht hat" ("a Mount of Olives, which has been used on the New Market") and

---

31. "Das Spiel der Ausführung Christi bei St. Stephan in Wien," in *Jahrbuch der Gesellschaft für Wiener Theaterforschung 1945–1946* (Vienna, 1946), pp. 116–57.

"eine Sayln zu der Gaislung des Hergots" ("a column for the scourging of the Lord").[32]

Now Rollinger was not only the Regierer: he had woodcarving as his principal occupation, and in this capacity participated in the work on the artistic details of the old choir stalls in Saint Stephan's Cathedral. The theme of this magnificent piece of carving was the Passion of Christ. Two scholars have concerned themselves with this duality of Rollinger's functions, Hans Rupprich[33] and Heinz Kindermann.[34] Rupprich intoned the melody and Kindermann joined in. We should like to examine this remarkable Rollinger case more closely.

The choir stalls, destroyed by fire in April 1945,[35] had forty-six scenes from the Old and New Testaments, of which four were substitutions made during the Baroque period. Thus, forty-two of the reliefs were Gothic, most of them carved out of linden wood. Their average size was fifty-eight by fifty-eight centimeters. Art historians attributed thirty-three reliefs to master craftsmen, while nine were regarded as the work of journeymen. There is no doubt about Rollinger's share in the carvings, although it can no longer be determined how many of the reliefs are from his hand. He worked together with other masters between 1476 and 1486/87 (and perhaps longer) on the story of Christ's Passion, carved in wood. The scenes of the reliefs coincide with the putative scenes of the Viennese Passion Play. On this point Rupprich observes, "It is hardly an accident, after all, but rather proves the very strongest dependence of the choir stalls' passion reliefs upon the passion performances which had been viewed on the stage."[36] And then Kindermann: "It is certainly no accident, but rather proves only the strong dependence of Rollinger's passion reliefs on those scenic happenings which Rollinger had arranged and observed on stages (mansions)."[37] Rupprich continues, "Thus, here in Vienna, we are confronted with a unique case of the closest sort of connection between pictorial and theatrical art, so that an important late-medieval master also carried out the staging of passion plays at the very church for which he created his wood carvings."[38] Kindermann scarcely

32. Ibid., p. 138.
33. "Das Wiener Schrifttum des ausgehenden Mittelalters," *Sitzungsberichte der Österreichischen Akademie der Wissenschaften*, Phil.-hist. Kl. vol. 208 (1954).
34. *Theatergeschichte Europas*, 1:263.
35. Lucca Chmel photographed the reliefs shortly before they were consumed by fire; Paul Stix edited the photographs in *Die Wiener Passion* (Vienna, 1950).
36. "Das Wiener Schrifttum," p. 124.
37. *Theatergeschichte Europas*, 1:263.
38. "Das Wiener Schrifttum," p. 124. This passage also occurs in almost identical form in Rupprich's "Das mittelalterliche Schauspiel in Wien," *Jahrbuch der Grillparzer-Gesellschaft*, n. s., 3 (1943): 45.

Christ being led captive into Jerusalem. Woodcarving (by Wilhelm Rollinger?) from the choir stalls of Saint Stephen's Cathedral, Vienna. The original was destroyed in World War II, shortly after this photograph was taken by Lucca Chmel. Excellent reproductions of all the lost carvings may be found in Paul Stix, ed., *Die Wiener Passion* (Vienna, 1950).

Pilate washes his hands. Woodcarving (by Wilhelm Rollinger?) from the choir stalls of Saint Stephen's Cathedral, Vienna. Courtesy of Herold Verlag, Vienna.

varied the sentence at all, and, convinced of the identity of Viennese sculpture and Viennese stage, rejoiced at the sight of the wood carvings: "At last, we know now the gate of Pilate's house, at last, we recognize the throne room of Herod; we know how the column looked at which the scourging was carried out; we recognize the stylized, three-level scenery with rocks and landscapes, the profiles of city walls, of which Rollinger made use."[39]—Kindermann means, of course, Rollinger the stage director. But, by all means, let us come down to earth. The house of Pilate was to be seen on six of the reliefs. However, it was the same house only in quite a general sense. Variations could be detected in the details, variations dictated by the conscience of the pictorial artist. For example, the stairway, which is on the viewer's right in five instances, in the sixth (Jesus sent to Herod by Pilate) is moved to the left of the picture. For reasons of space, the window in which Pilate twice shows himself is transformed, during the scene where the Governor washes his hands, into a sort of platform. Likewise, we do not "recognize" the throne of Herod. The "throne room" consists simply of a chair before a background of round and pointed arches. On the relief, the column for the scourging is nothing more than the supporting pillar of a vaulted arch and certainly bears no resemblance to the "Sayln zu der Gaislung" in the inventory of the Brotherhood. The "profiles of city walls" in the reliefs are simply devices used by the pictorial artist for overcoming the problem of perspective. It should not be assumed that, by means of "stage scaffolds," Rollinger transformed the streets of Vienna, from the New Market to Saint Stephan's, into a realistic *via crucis*. The "Ölperg" of the inventory surely bore no resemblance to Rollinger's Mount of Olives, rendered in wood by the artist on the basis of considerations having solely to do with pictorial composition. For a reconstruction of the "stage setting," a study of the reliefs is utterly unproductive—not to mention the fact that we lack a text.

It would also be inappropriate if, from the wood carvings, we attempted to draw conclusions about the language of gestures used in the play. Rollinger (and his colleagues) gave their carved figures movements and mimetic expressions in accordance with the dictates of their artistic imagination. Rollinger could not expect, at any event, that his lay actors, technically unschooled as they were, could abandon themselves to their roles with such intensity. Petersen had already called for moderation in his first Frankfurt lecture: "An effort to measure the mimetic accomplishments of the medieval actor's art against the spiritual expressivity of the Gothic style appears

39. *Theatergeschichte Europas*, 1:263.

to be particularly inadmissible. We shall never know to what degree the performance exceeded wooden clumsiness and dilettantish exaggeration."[40]

With regard to the costuming, we may well think of elements held in common by stage and image. Surely Rollinger did not costume his actors any differently than he did the figures in his reliefs. The assumption is altogether rational. But, in this instance too, the carvings are of no more help to us than the inventory. That Annas was supplied with a miter can also be learned from the documents published by Capra,[41] where "ain Inoffel als ain Pischoff" ("a miter like a bishop's") is set aside for Annas. That Pilate was dressed in "türkischart" ("Turkish fashion") is something the inventory tells us more readily than the reliefs do. That Herod bore a "kuphren vergult Zepter") ("a guilded scepter of copper") and a "kuphren Appfl" ("a copper apple") as his insignia is evident from the inventory alone. The reliefs yield nothing more on this point. The inventory is more informative for the simple reason that it tells us about colors, information which the wood carvings keeps from us. Thus a "weisser mantl" ("white cloak") was intended for John, and, for the Savior in the Ecce-homo scene, a "roter Zendlpostmantl" ("red taffeta cloak"). The leader of the Synagogue wore a "gelber leynen manntl gemösert" ("yellow spotted linen cloak"). The hats of the Jews were made out of paper, a fact which the reliefs conceal. In other words, lacking photographs of the reliefs, we would not be less well informed about the details of the Viennese performance. At the New Market, Rollinger was the Regierer; in his workshop he was a pictorial artist.

"THE MARTYRDOM OF SAINT APOLLONIA"

In the book of hours which Jehan Fouquet illuminated for Etienne Chevalier around 1460 there is a miniature which provides a unique document for the theater historian, the torture of Saint Apollonia presented in a theatrical context. We do not possess another record of the same sort. Unhappily, the play has not survived upon which the miniature was based. In short, we have a pictorial document, but no text. Can we reconstruct the performance? By no means. We do not know how much time the dramatist spent with the events leading up to the martyrdom, and so we do not know at what juncture in the play the torture, depicted here, took place, nor do we know what followed it. The Lübeck Passional offers what is probably the most extensive account of this holy legend. Apollonia was tortured a number of times. Fouquet portrayed only one torture, the extraction of her teeth with a pair of huge

40. *Das deutsche Nationaltheater,* p. 16.
41. "Das Spiel der Ausführung Christi," p. 140.

forceps. Cohen[42] (following Bapst) thought that her tongue was being pulled out, a harmless confusion of Apollonia's fate with the martyrdom of Saint Livinus. But since faithful folk suffering from toothache turned to Saint Apollonia for succor, we may assume that the author and Fouquet clung to this tradition.

In his picture the artist gave permanence to what he obviously had seen in the theater: six mansions on pilings one story high, arranged in a half-circle or half-oval around a central acting area (platea). Four of these mansions have a clear-cut function: Heaven with God the Father and the angels, Hell opposite; further, the loge for the orchestra and in the center the mansion of the emperor (Decius?), who has left his throne in order to watch the torture close at hand. Two mansions are ambivalent. Next to the imperial loge we see ladies in fashionable dress, and beside Hell there are women of a more bourgeois appearance. Cohen thought that they were privileged spectators, while the male public was thronged beneath the elevated mansions. In each of the two ladies' loges an amorous couple amuses itself, plainly bored with the events on stage. There is no way to reach the platea from these two loges, but Heaven is connected with earth by a sort of primitive duckboard, and access to the imperial loge is provided by a simple ladder, aided by which the emperor must have descended from his throne, albeit not in a very dignified fashion. Fouquet so arranged the central action that Etienne Chevalier was afforded an unobstructed view of the torture scene. (The artist did the same thing with the torture of other saints—the stoning of Saint Stephan, the beheading of Saint James, and the crucifixion of Saint Andrew.) The picture of Apollonia gets an unimpeachably theatrical quality through the presence of the meneur de jeu and of the man with blue trousers, trousers he has dropped in order to present his naked backside both to the saint and the pious Chevalier.

The miniature offers more riddles than it solves, for the simple reason that we do not have the text of the miracle play. In case additional stage locations were required, the half-circle would have had to be expanded to a full one, and then we should have been confronted with a clear instance of a circular theater. The public, beneath the mansions, would surround the platea. This was Cohen's argument in his introduction to the Mons documents. He called our attention to the man at the left of Paradise, who props himself with his arms against a crossbeam, attentively following the action on the platea. In this Cohen saw the beginning of an "autre hémicycle, composé probablement de galeries, réservées aux spectateurs, peut-être d'autres mansions."[43] The whole design reminded him of a Roman circus.

42. Études d'histoire du théâtre, p. 52.
43. Le livre de conduite, p. xlviii.

Without a text, we grope in the dark. The text alone could tell us whether still other mansions were required (in which case Fouquet portrayed only half the ring of mansions), or if we are justified in taking the open side as a space for the spectators—a space which, for the rest, did not absolutely need to be circular but which guaranteed the public a free view of the events on the stage. The crowd which the painter shoved in beneath the mansions may have been extras; as spectators, under the conditions presented in the picture, they would have seen nothing of the torture. Natalie Crohn Schmitt made this observation: "The arrangement of the actors is strongly frontal. If this were an accurate representation of performance, the audience shown—half the total audience by Southern's reckoning—could see nothing whatever of what seems to be the play's most dramatic moment."[44]

Richard Southern[45] has used the miniature as evidence for the erection of his theater-in-the-round—as a chief witness, so to speak, for his reconstruction of the performance of *The Castle of Perseverance.* His analysis of Fouquet's mansions and the component parts of their construction is expert and instructive. However, he also sought to cast some light on the decorative accessories which take up the lower part of the miniature, and, so doing, he arrived at some strange conclusions, conclusions influenced in part by his *idée fixe,* the *Castle* plan. To begin with, he rejected the notion of an elevated stage. Bapst was the first to have spoken of an "estrade—établie sur des fascines."[46] Decugis and Reymond[47] thought of a "scène circulaire," raised a meter above the ground and supported by bundles of sticks ("fagots," "fascines"). The hedge of intertwined branches which marks off the lower edge of the miniature has given rise to such fantasies as this. And Southern added another farfetched idea: in the basket-weave fence he perceived parts of a "barrier-fence," a fence designed to keep the nonpaying public from attending the play. I regard the "elevated stage" and the "non-elevated *platea* plus fence" as erroneous theories. In my opinion, the Fouquet fence is a piece of picturesque decoration, having no further significance. As far as the elevated stage is concerned, Crohn Schmitt has called attention to the fact that in other miniatures Fouquet likewise located the central action on a raised terrain, without our being permitted to assume that a stage action, of which Fouquet could have been an eyewitness, was once again involved. The martyrdoms of Saint Andrew and of Saint Catherine, the death of Peter on the cross,

44. "Was There a Medieval Theatre in the Round?," p. 21.
45. *The Medieval Theatre in the Round,* pp. 91–120.
46. Germain Bapst, *Essay sur l'histoire du théâtre* (Paris, 1893), p. 31.
47. Nicole Decugis and Suzanne Reymond, *Le décor de théâtre en France du Moyen Age à 1925* (Paris, 1953), p. 18.

and the conversion of Saul provide examples of this. In these cases we are confronted with a painter's compositional convention. I cannot take seriously Claude Schaefer's assertion that Fouquet was "a man of the theater" and that the theater "influenced the artist most strongly."[48] Richard Hosley,[49] who shares Southern's opinion that the miniature of Apollonia shows "a Place enclosed by a wattle fence," would like to introduce Fouquet's *Rape of the Sabine Women* in support of Southern's hypothesis, "a theatrical version of the rape of the Sabine women." Nevertheless, I can discover nothing pertaining to the theater in this miniature. Fouquet has placed the rape in an antique amphitheater, where, according to legend, the abduction is supposed to have taken place during a festival performance in honor of Neptune. The tiers from which Fouquet's Romans watched the spectacle have nothing in common with the scaffolds of Saint Apollonia.

48. Claude Schaefer, ed. *Jean Fouquet, the Hours of Etienne Chevalier* (New York, 1971), p. 22. Rey-Flaud, in *Le cercle magique,* is carried away by his boundless enthusiasm for the circular auditorium and finds theatrical echoes everywhere in Fouquet's miniatures. He calls the painter of the *Livre d'heures* an "homme de théâtre" (p. 113).

49. "Three Kinds of Outdoor Theatre before Shakespeare," p. 5. For a rejection of Hosley's view see Bamber Gascoigne, "Fouquet's 'Rape of the Sabine Women'," *Theatre Survey* 12 (November 1971): 155. Likewise unacceptable is Rey-Flaud's attempt (*Le cercle Magique,* pp. 134–36) to relate Fouquet's Roman amphitheater to the *Apollonia* miniature and the French medieval stage in general.

Index of Names